# Amazing Mandalas Coloring Book

*Copyright: Published in the United States by Christopher Bollinger*
*Published January 2017*
*ISBN-13: 978-1542679947*
*ISBN-10: 154267994X*

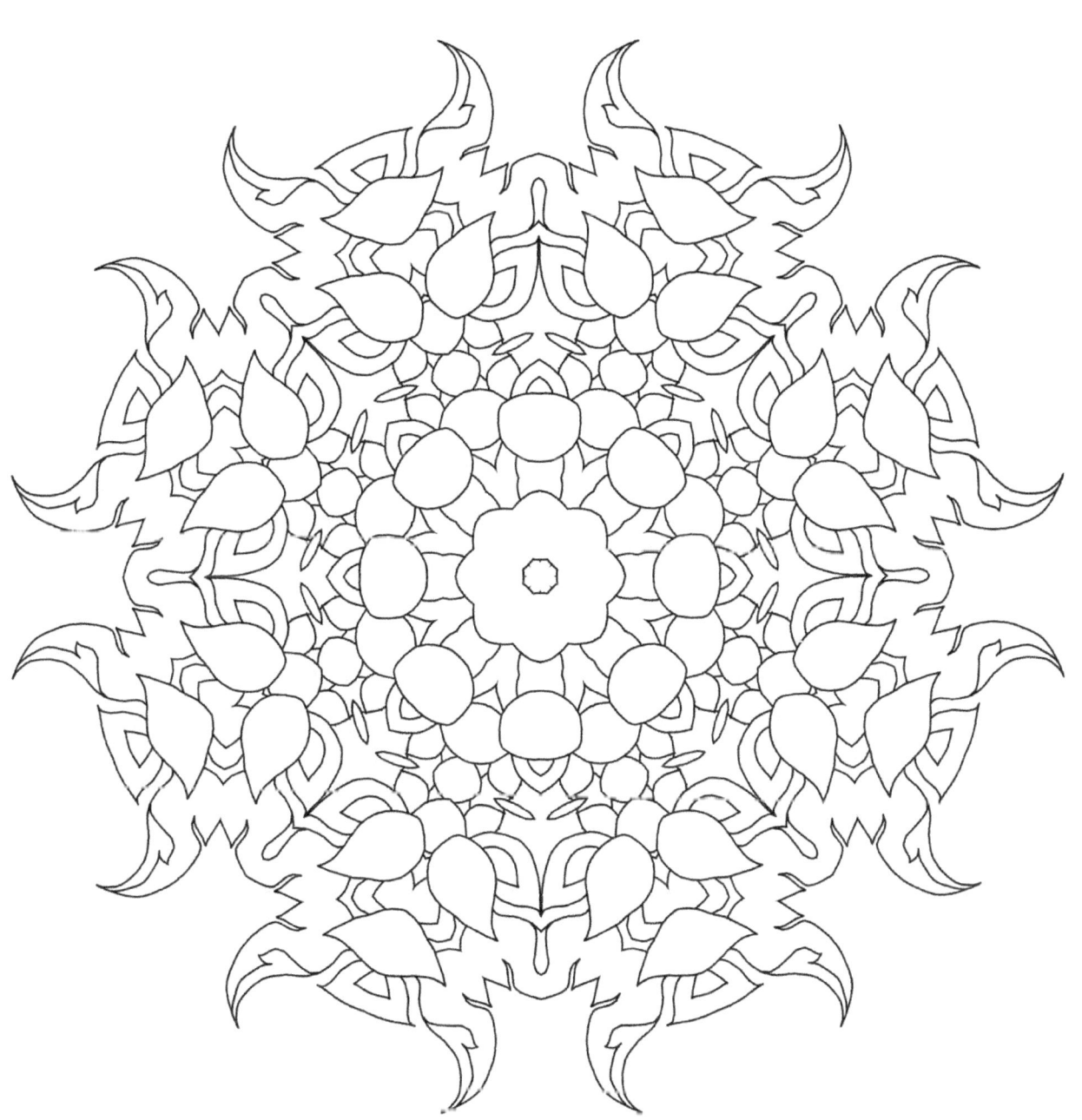

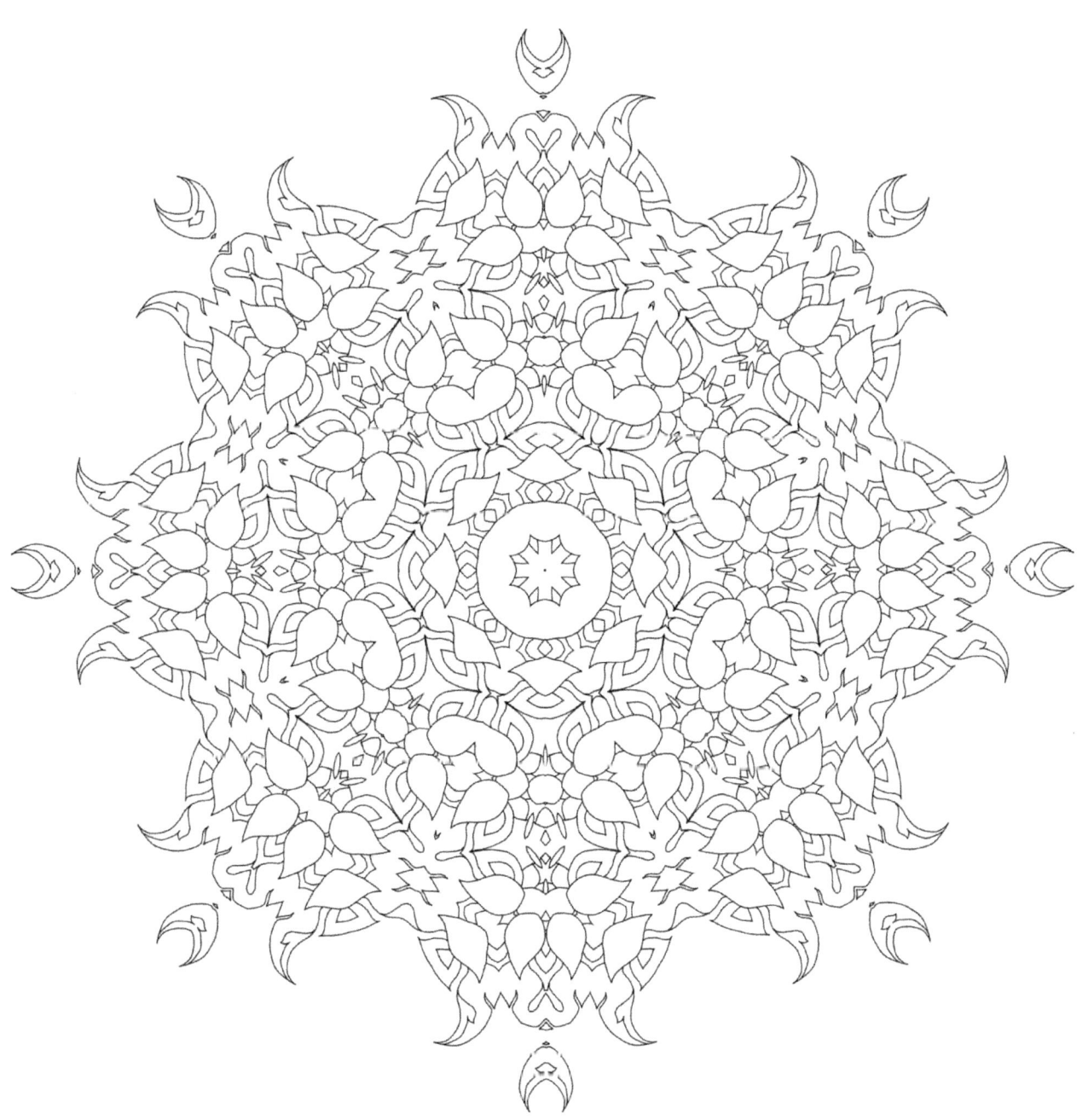

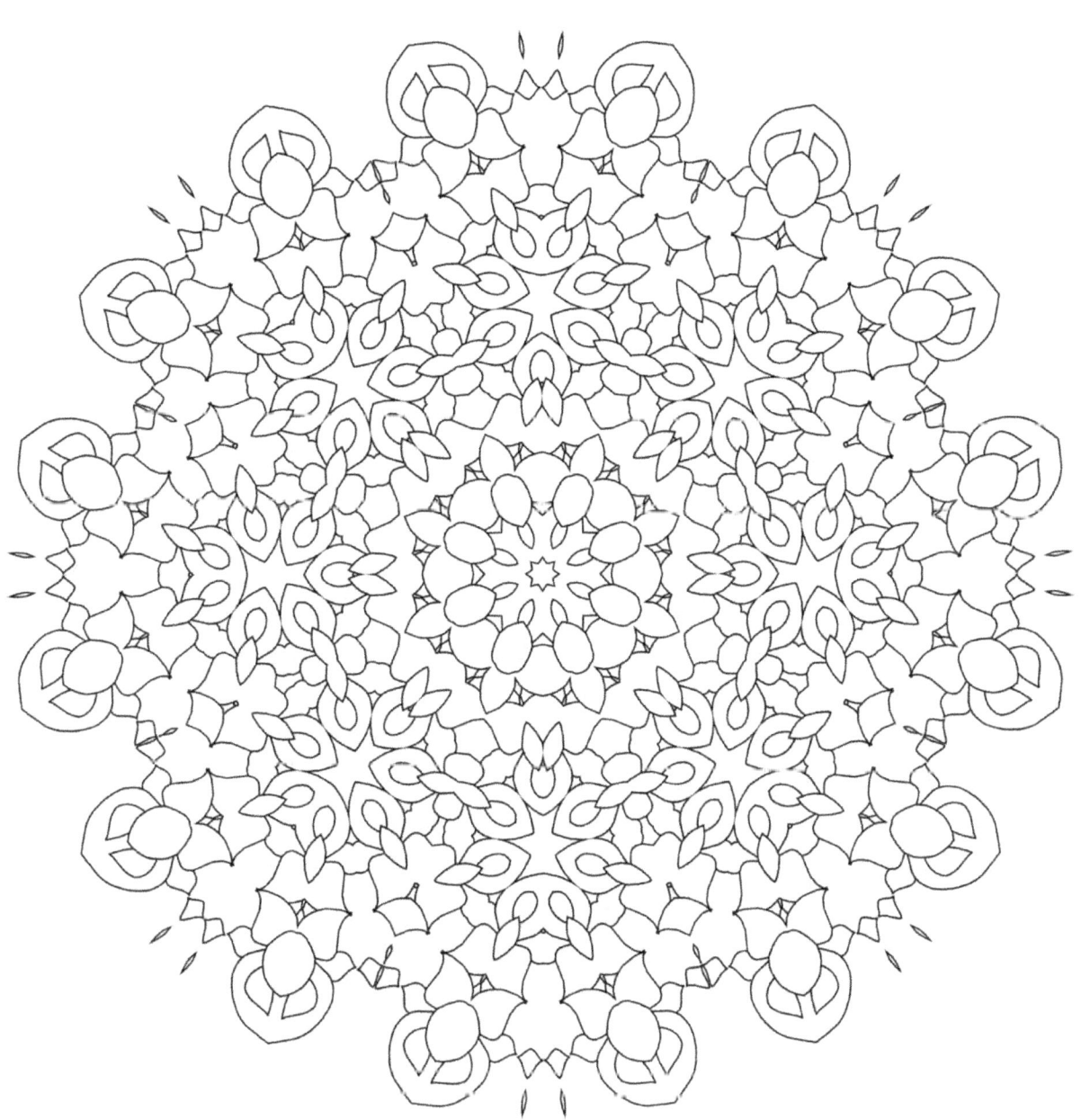

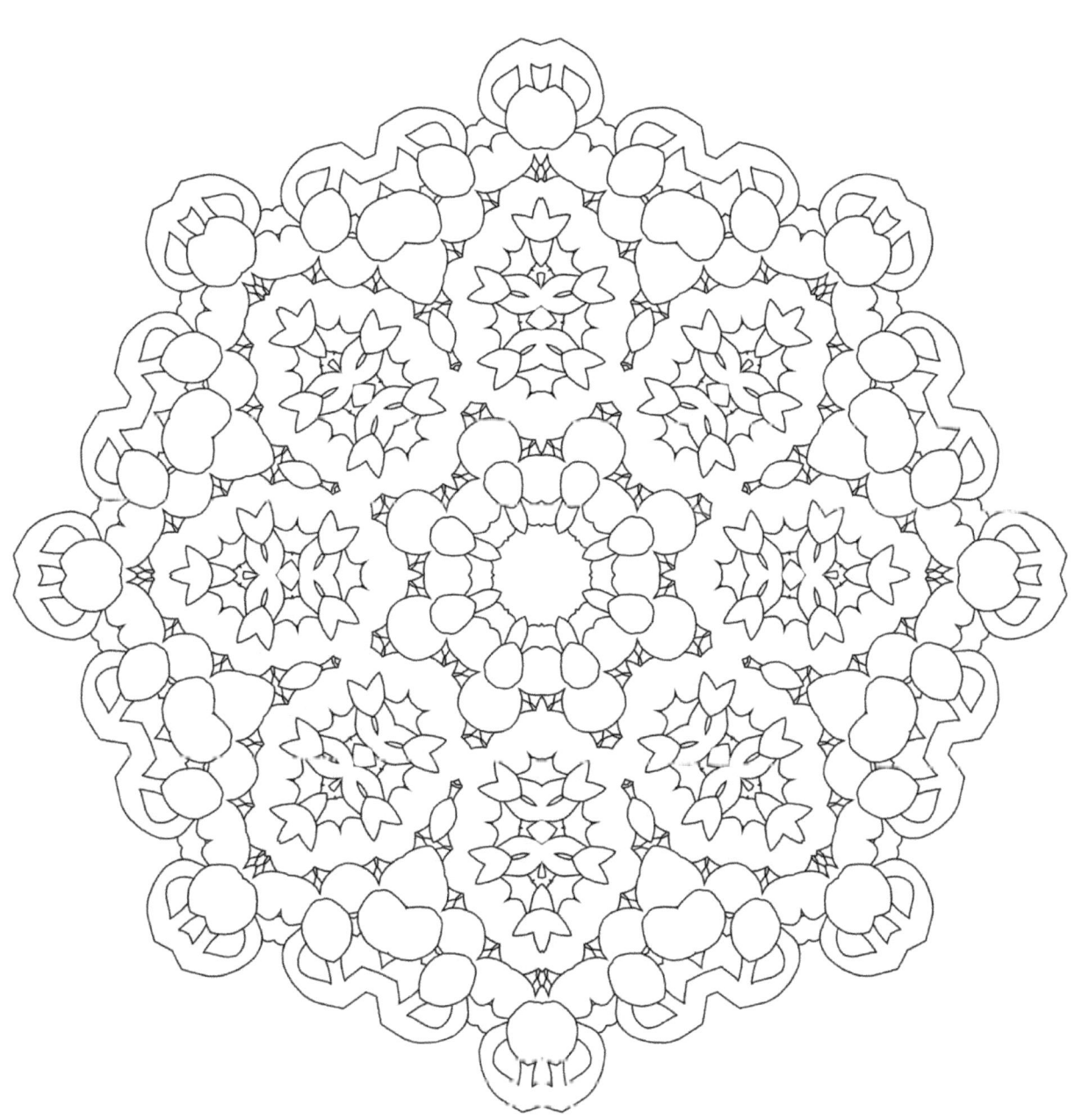

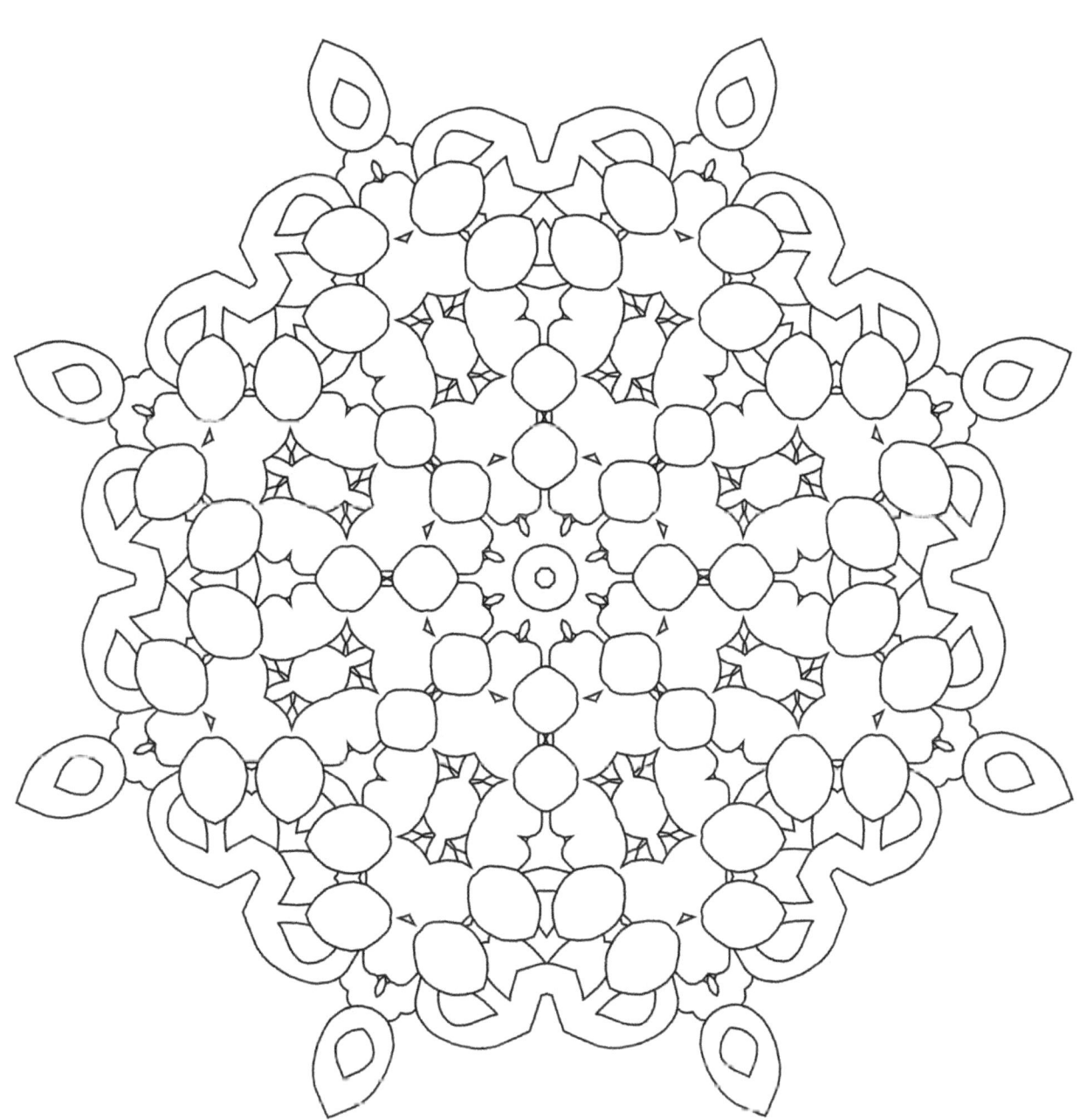

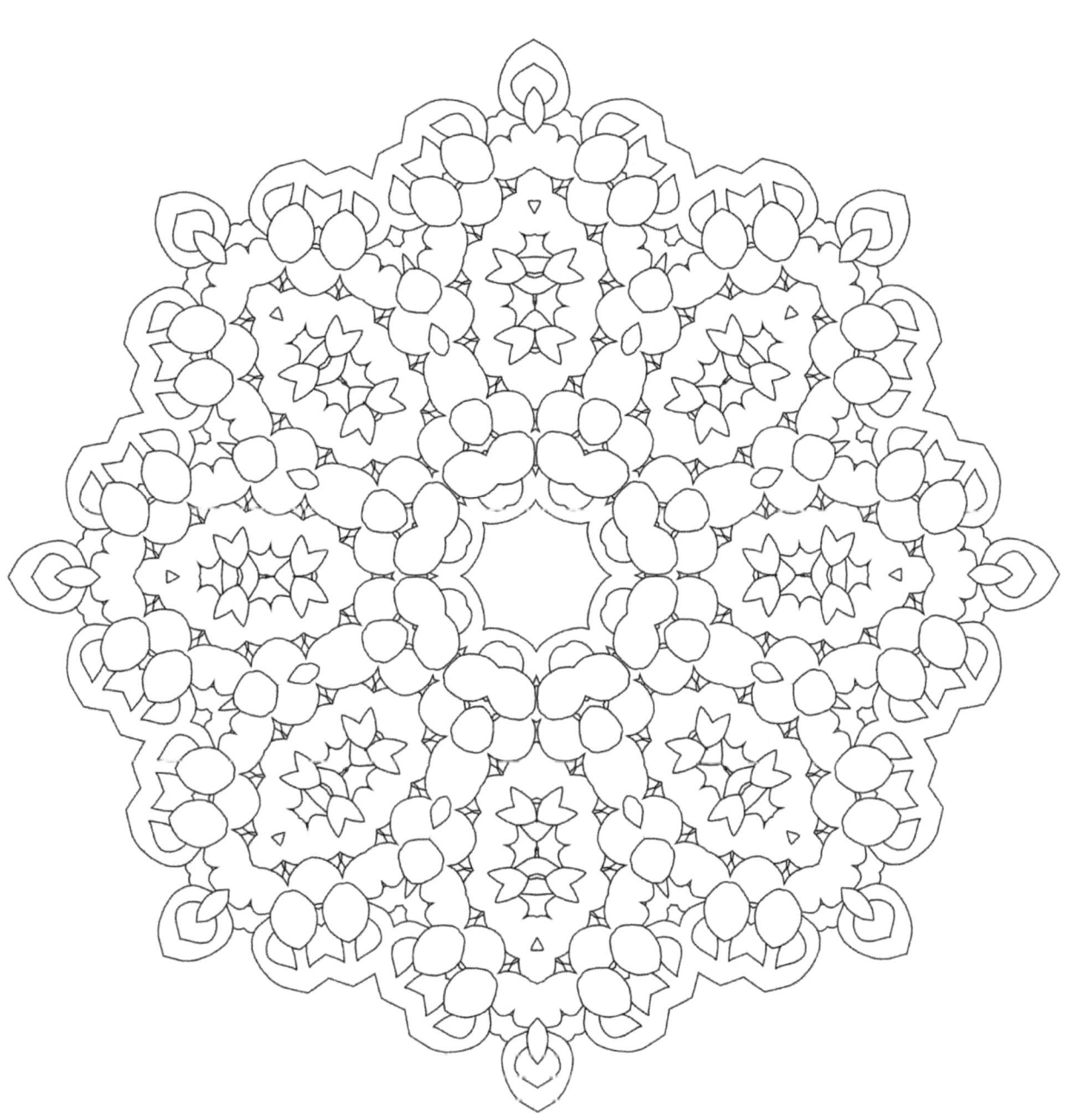

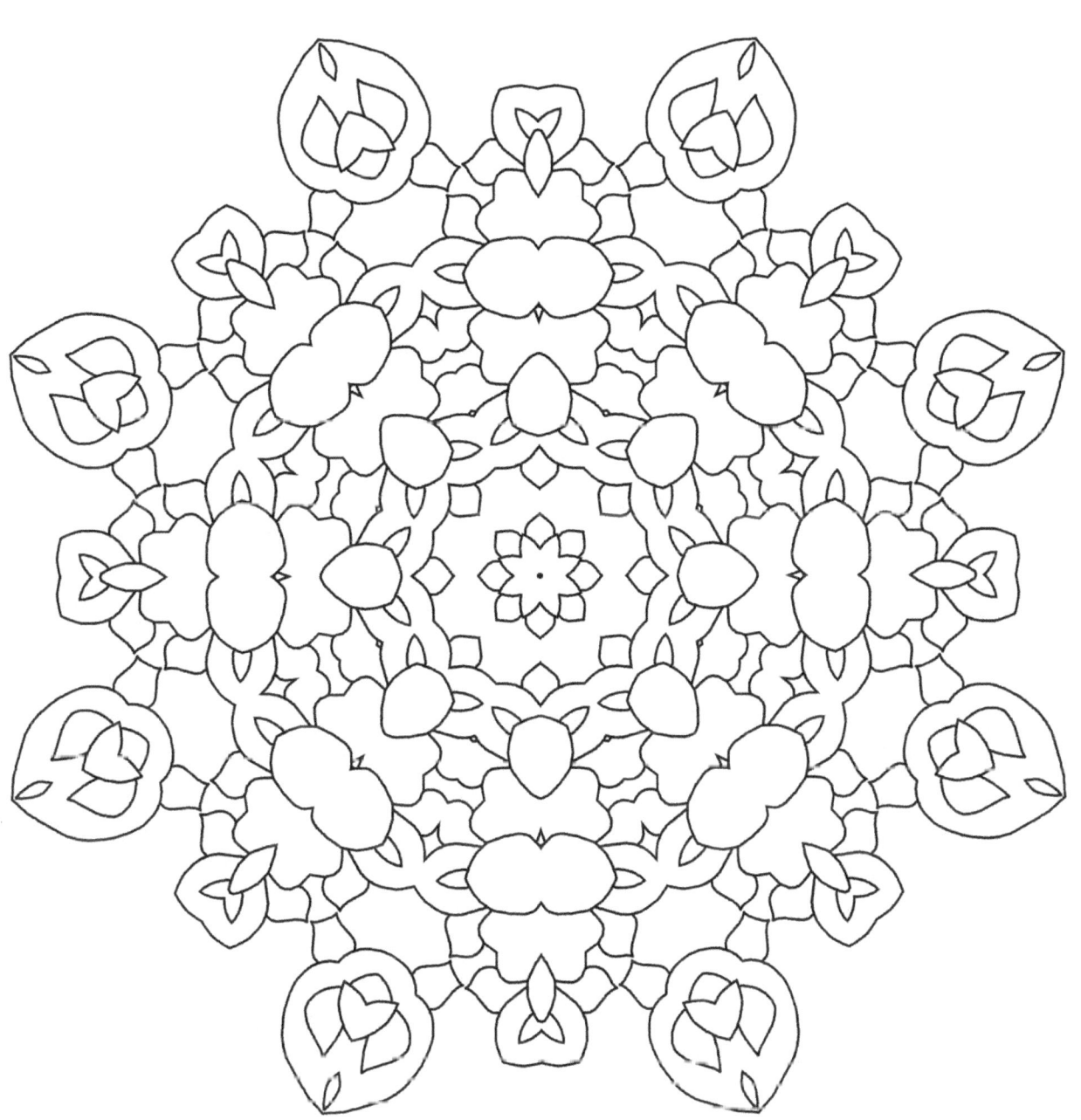

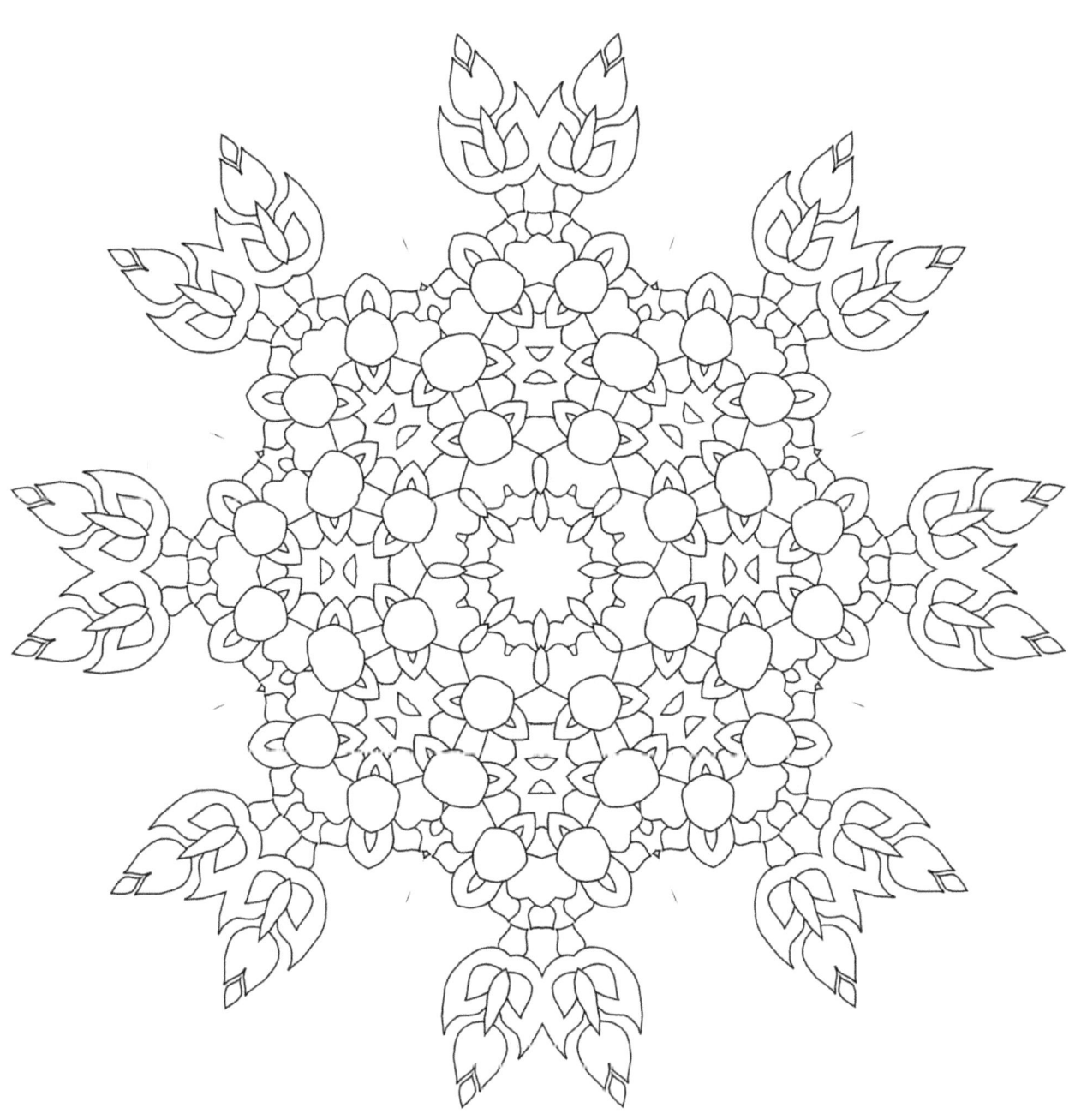

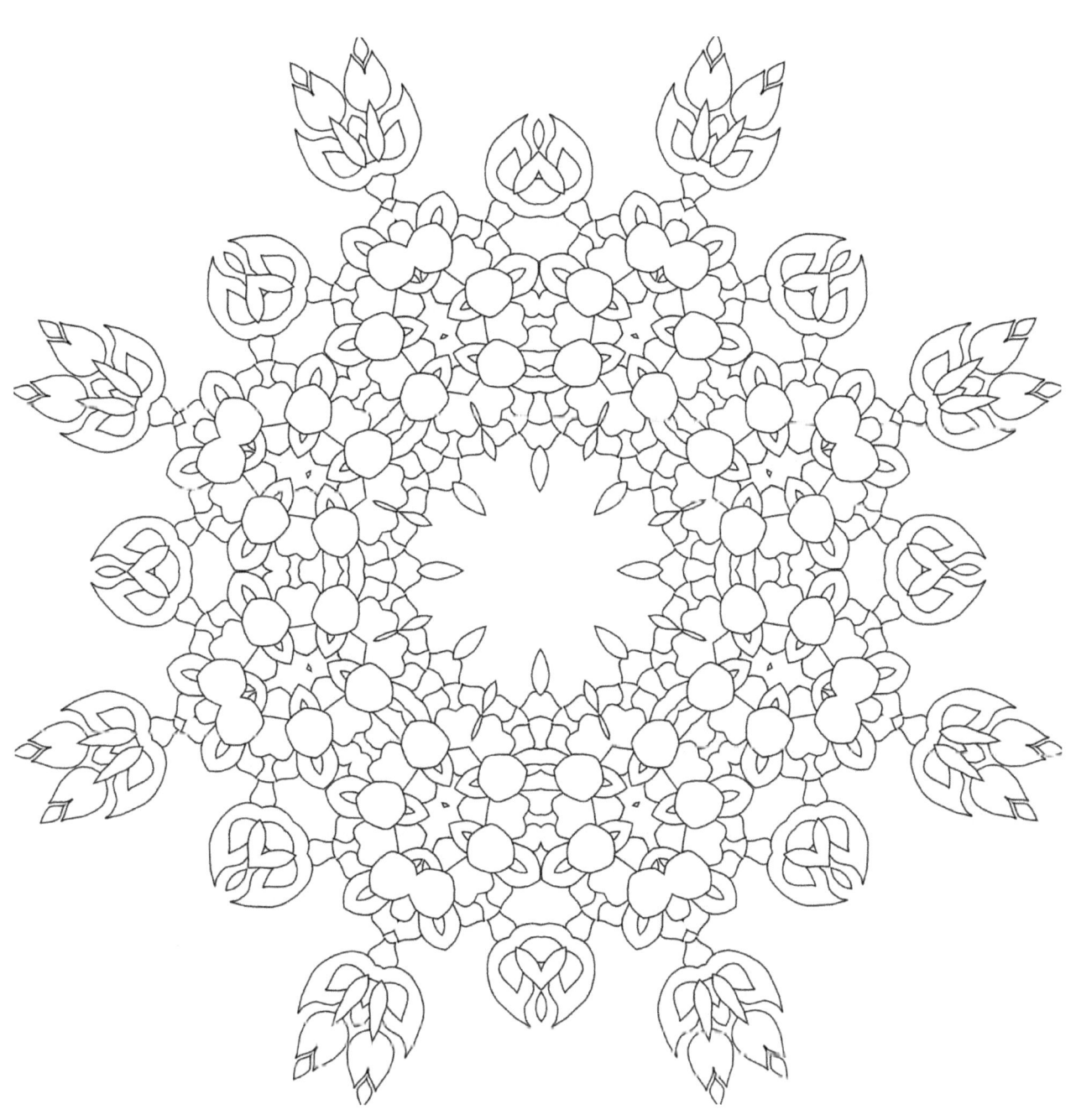

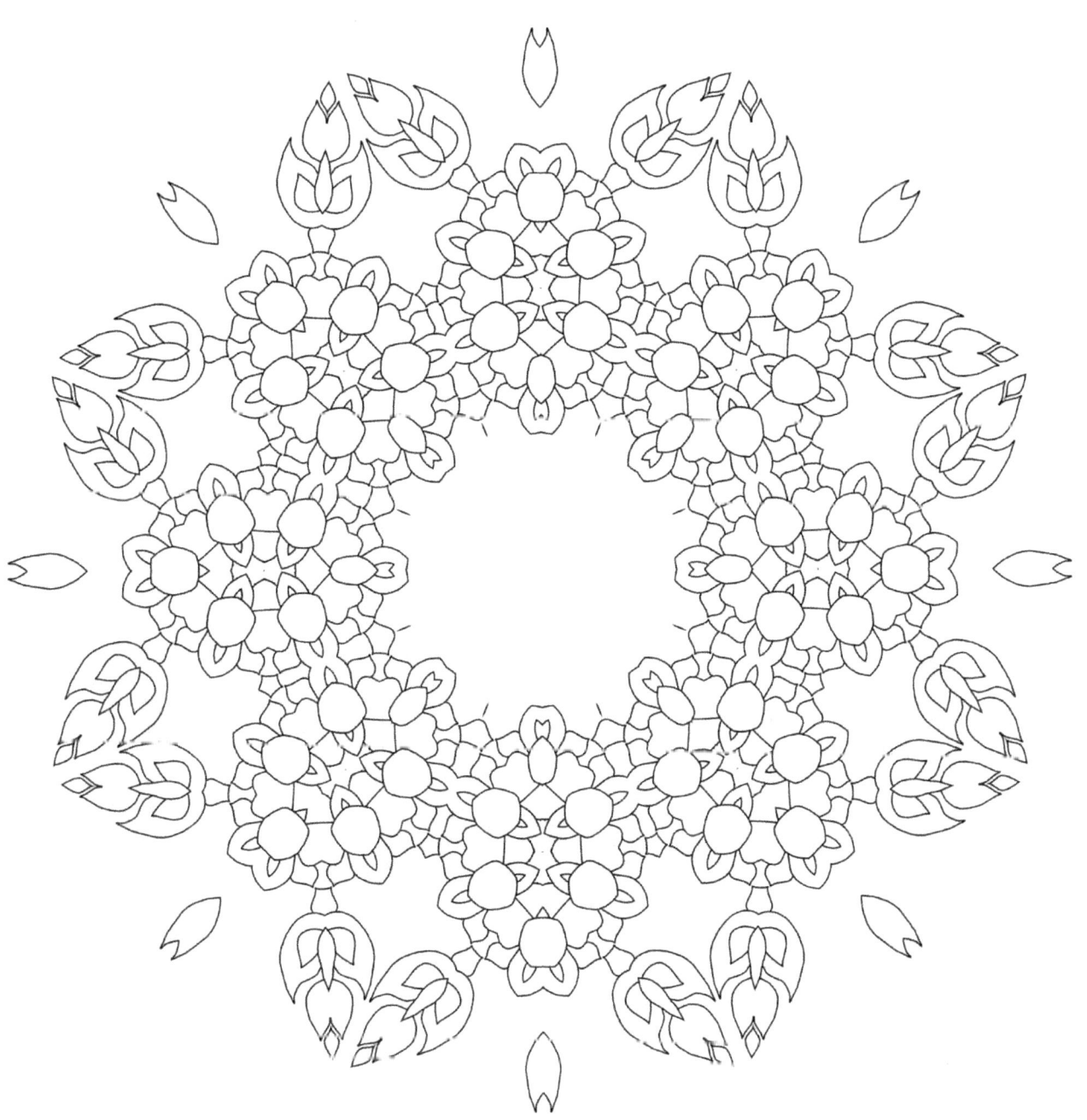

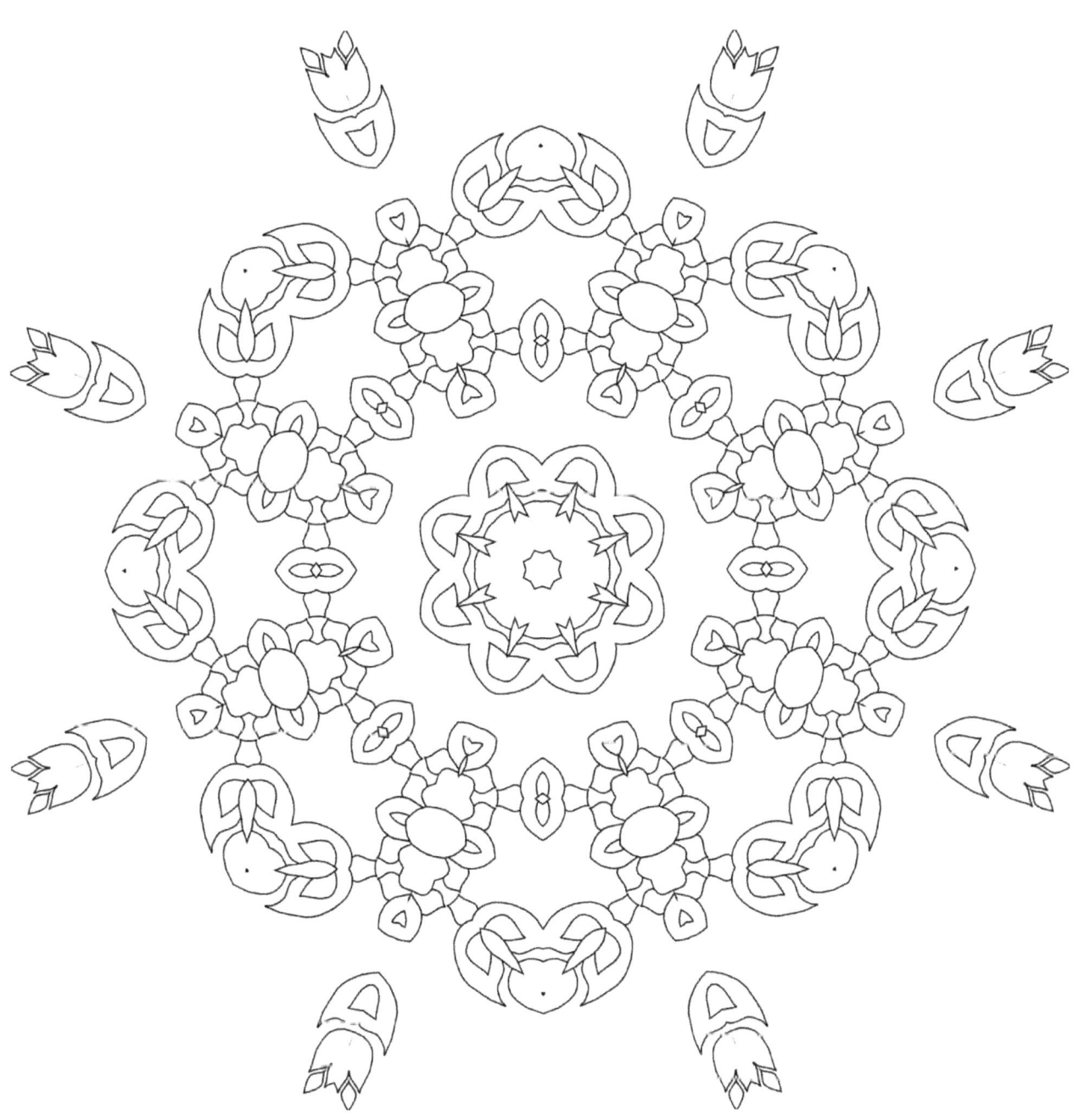

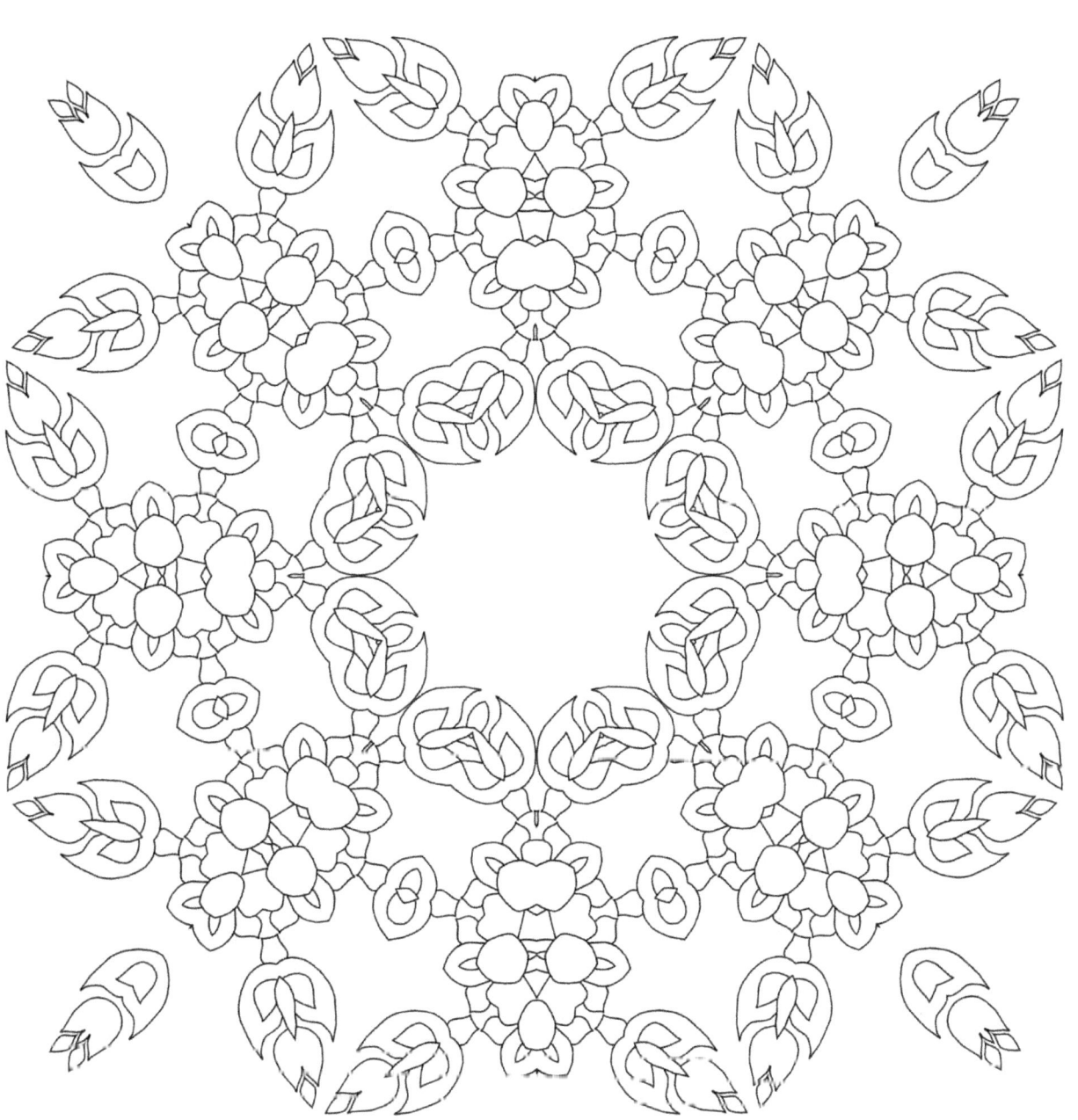

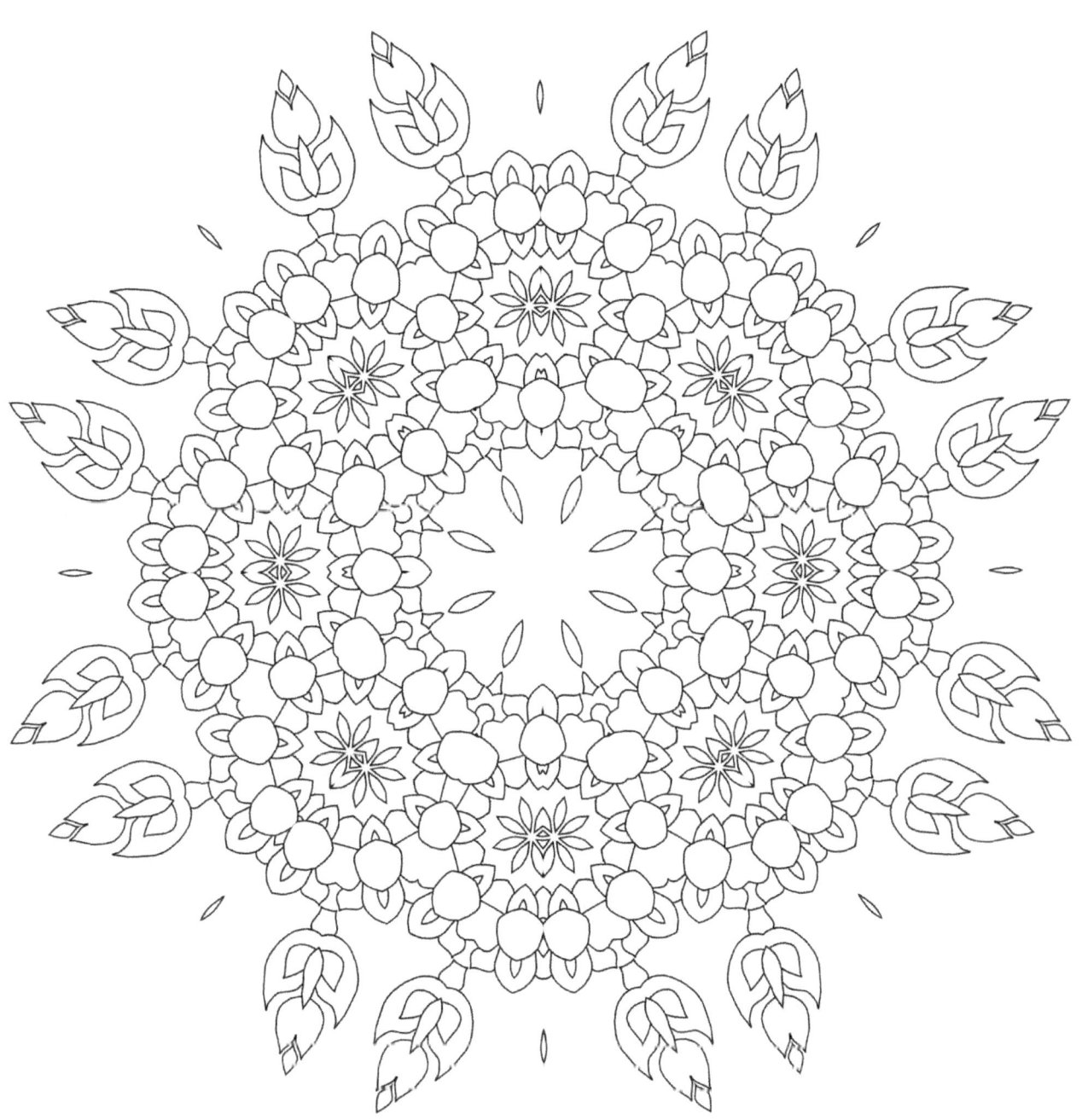

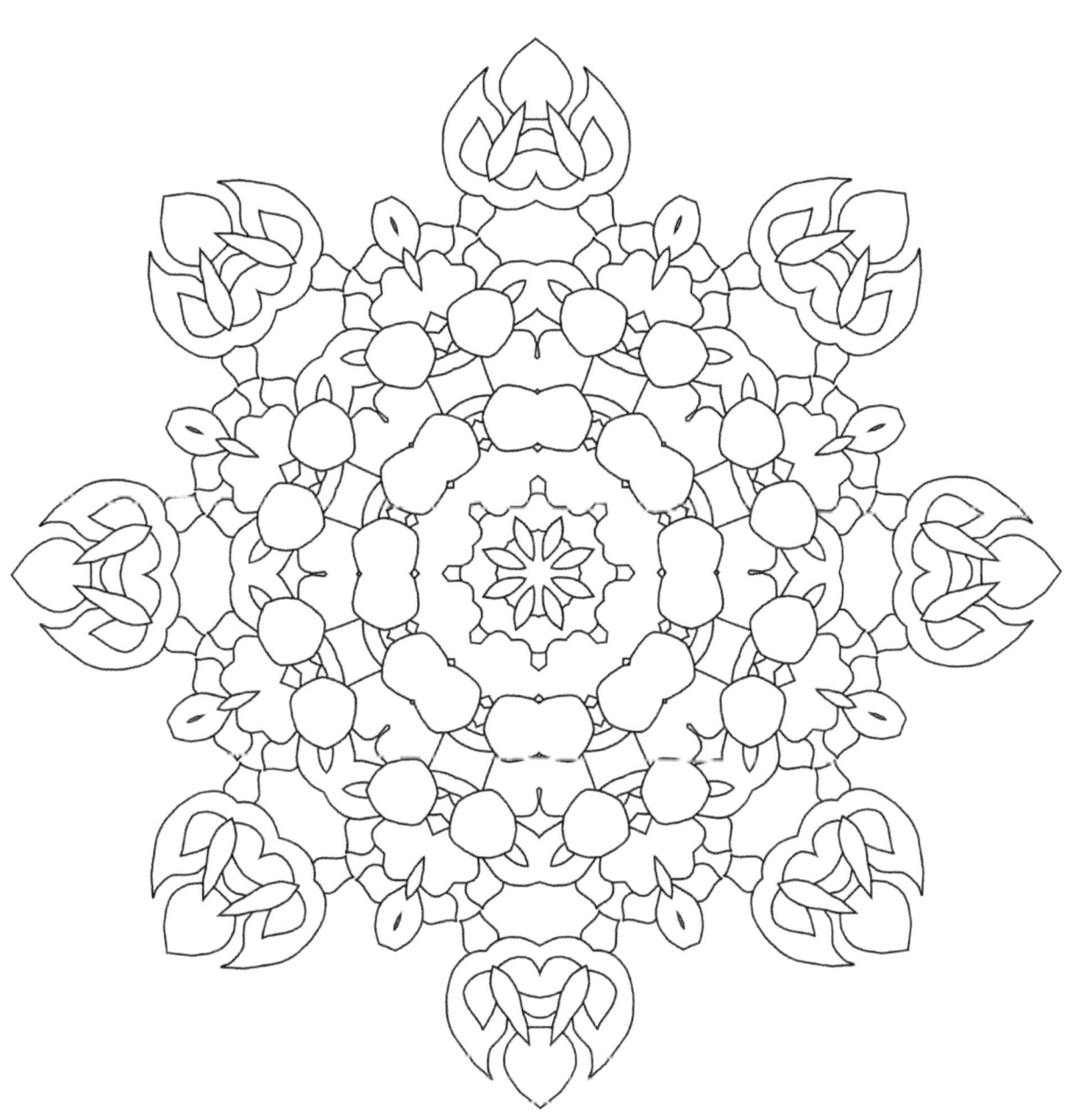

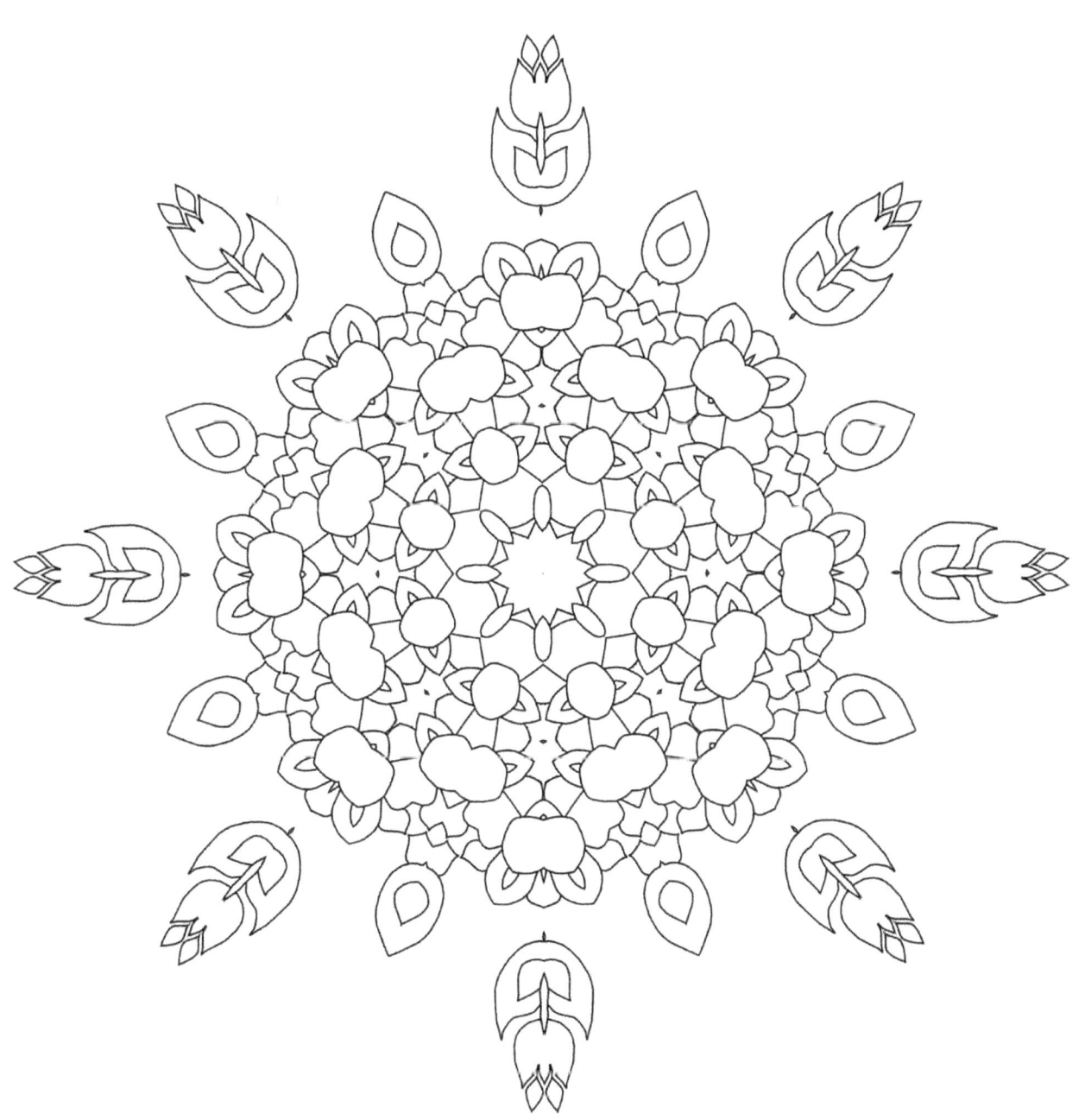

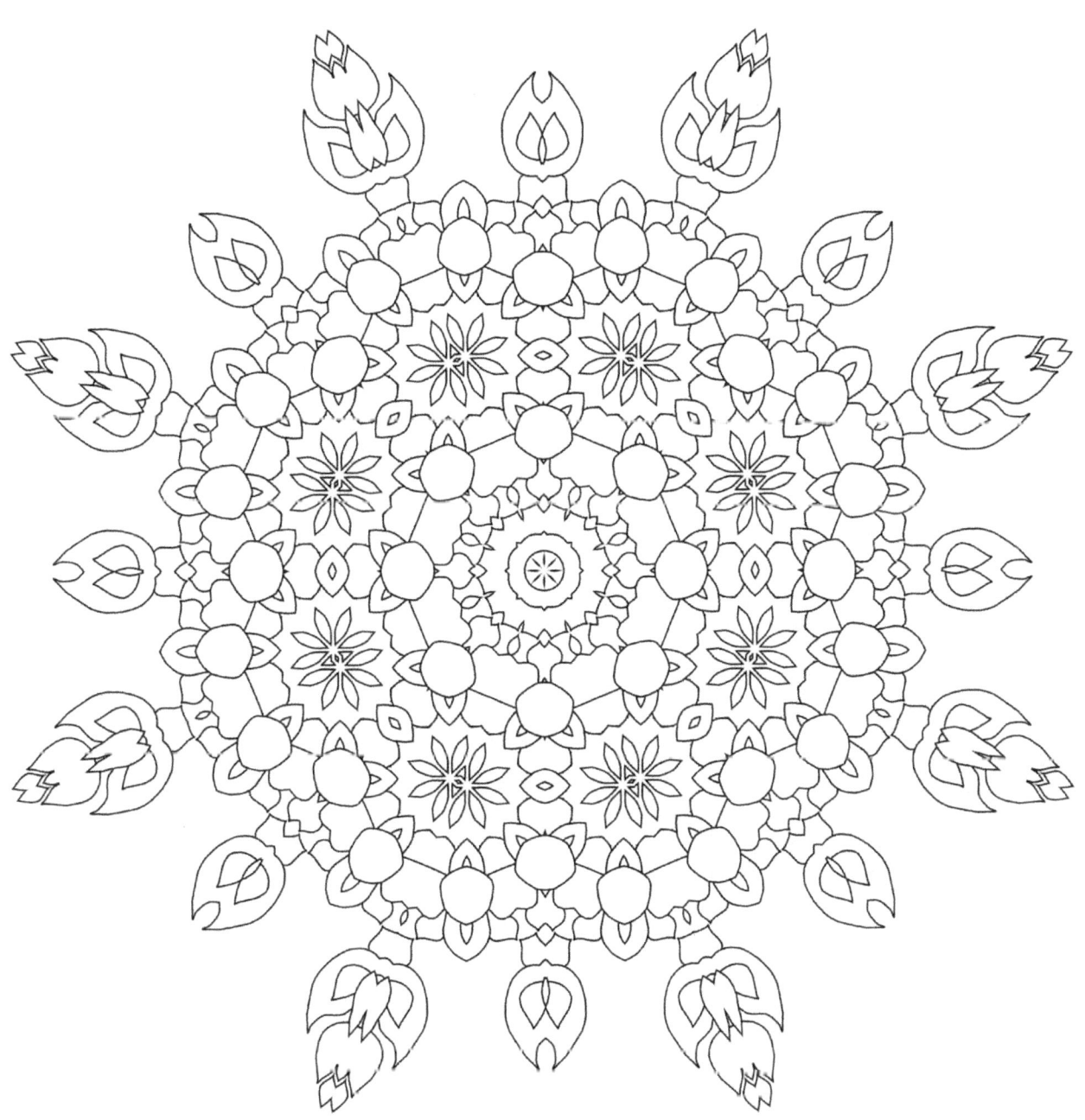

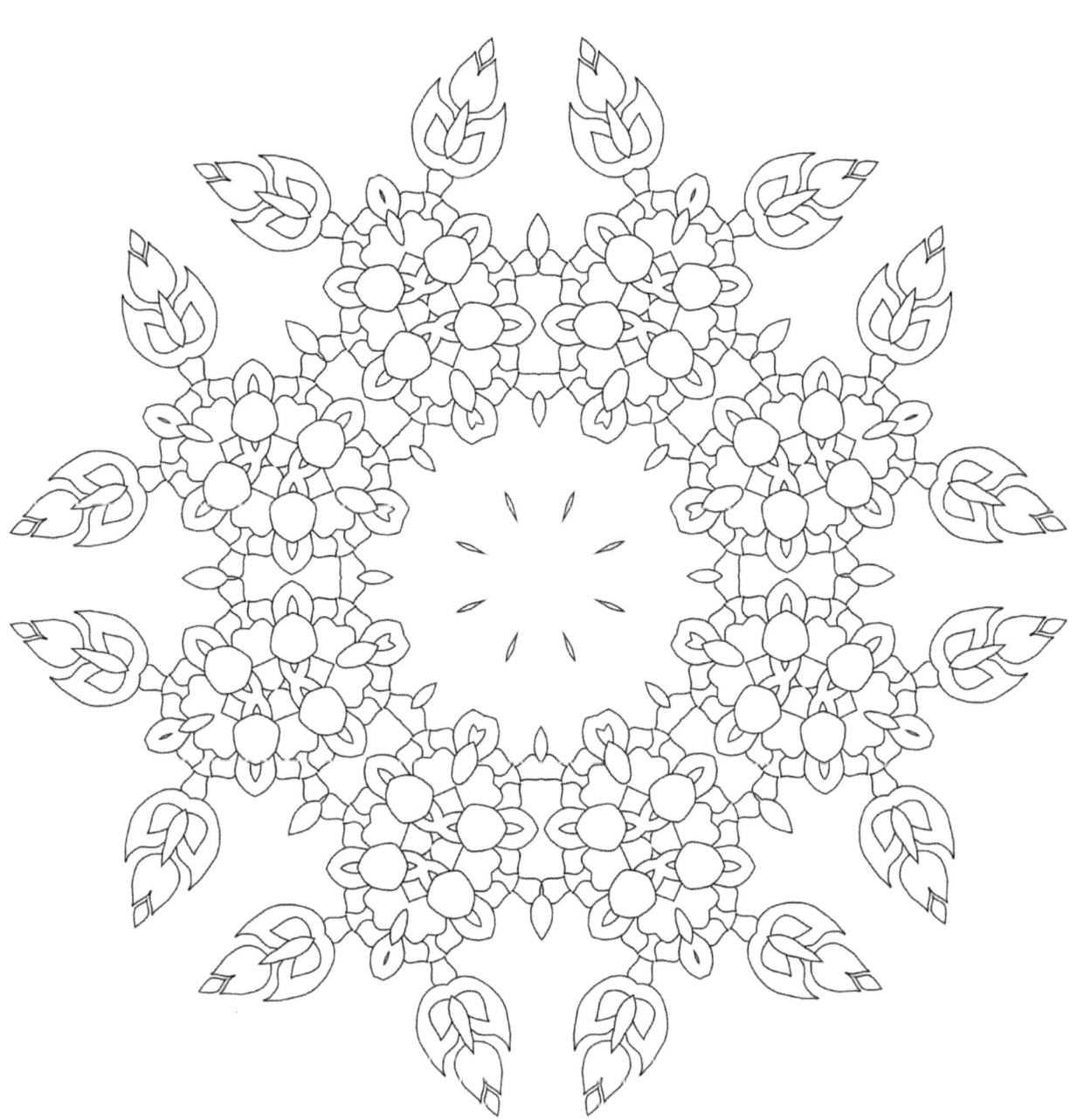

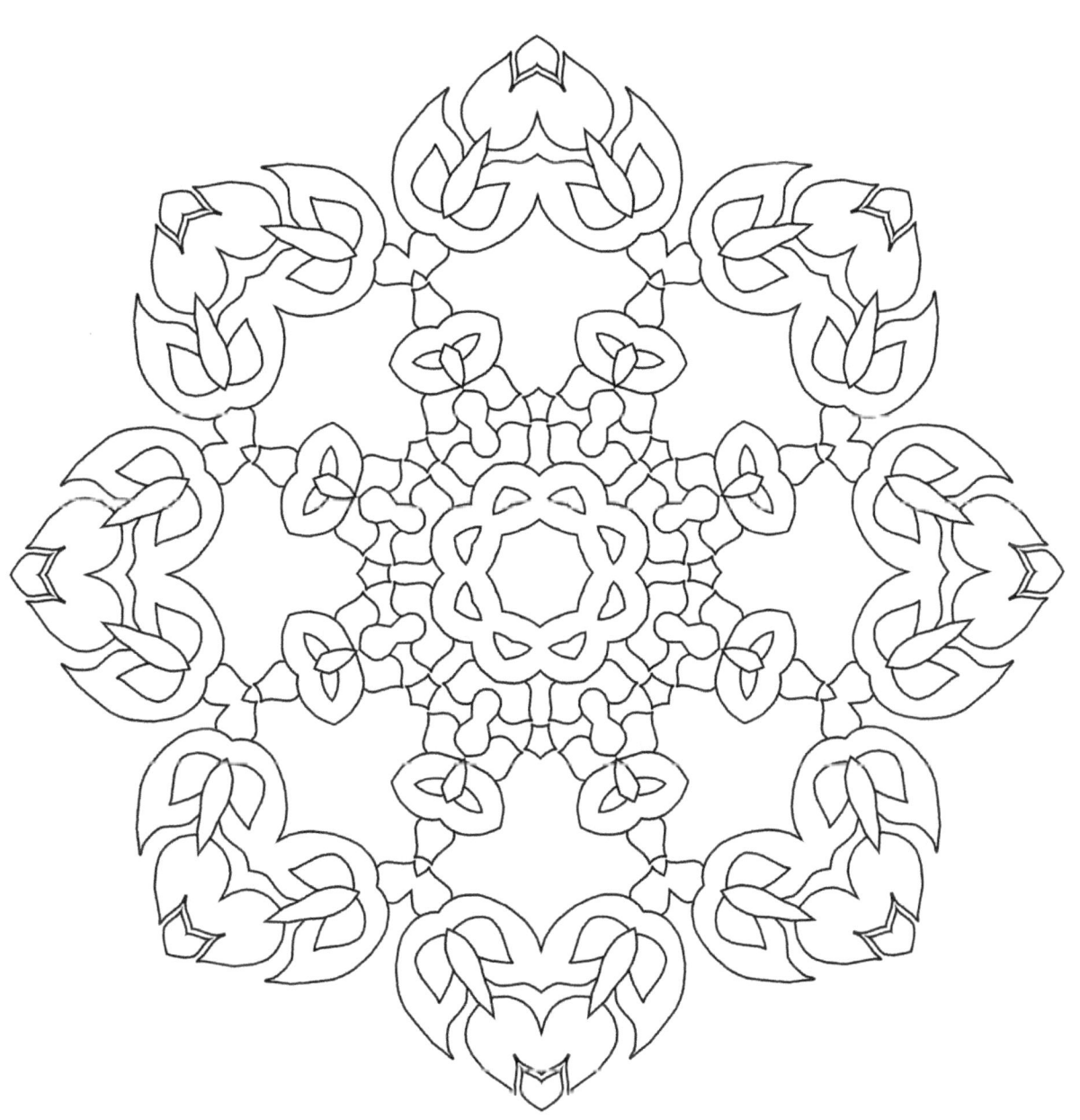

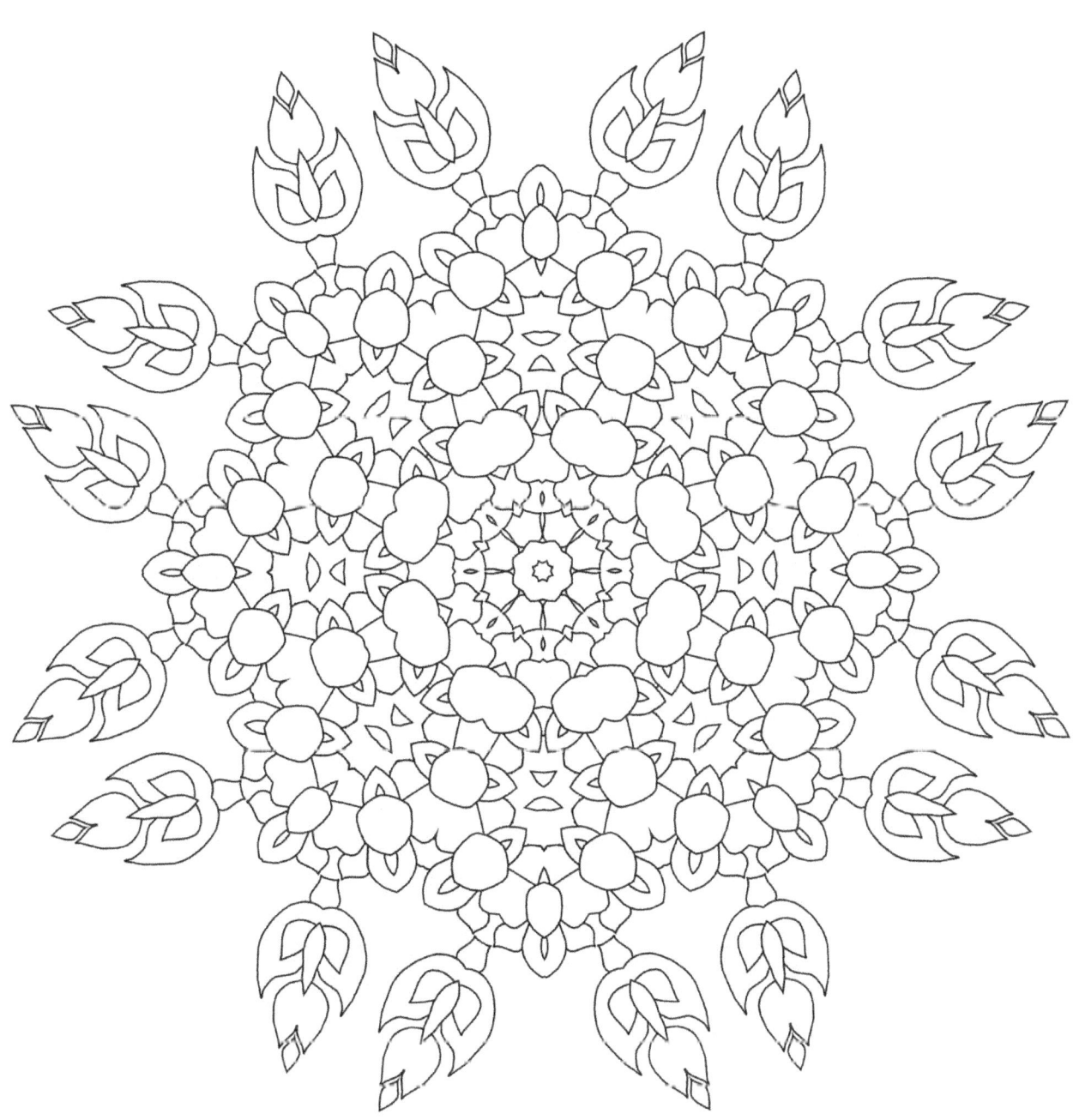

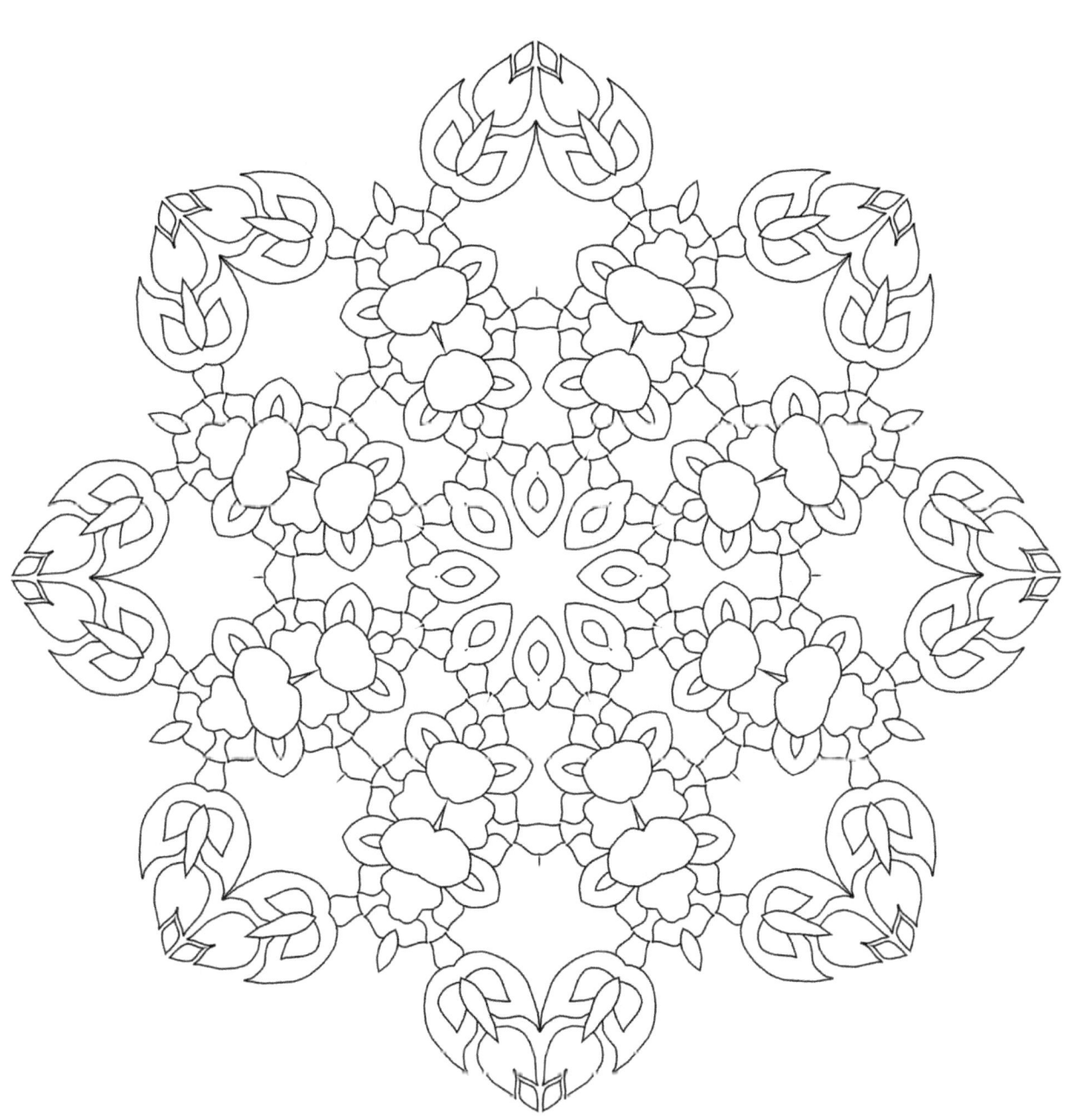

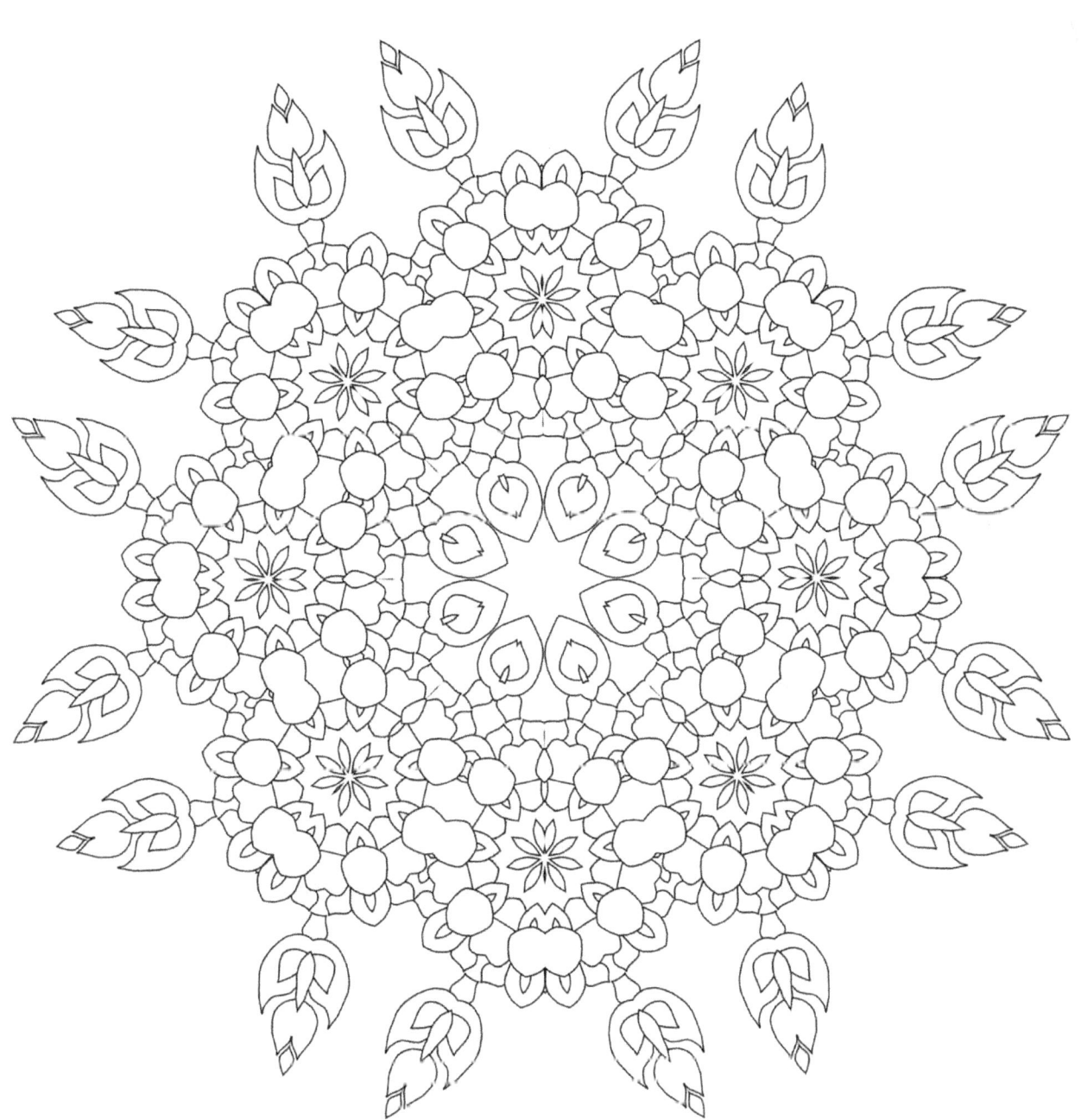

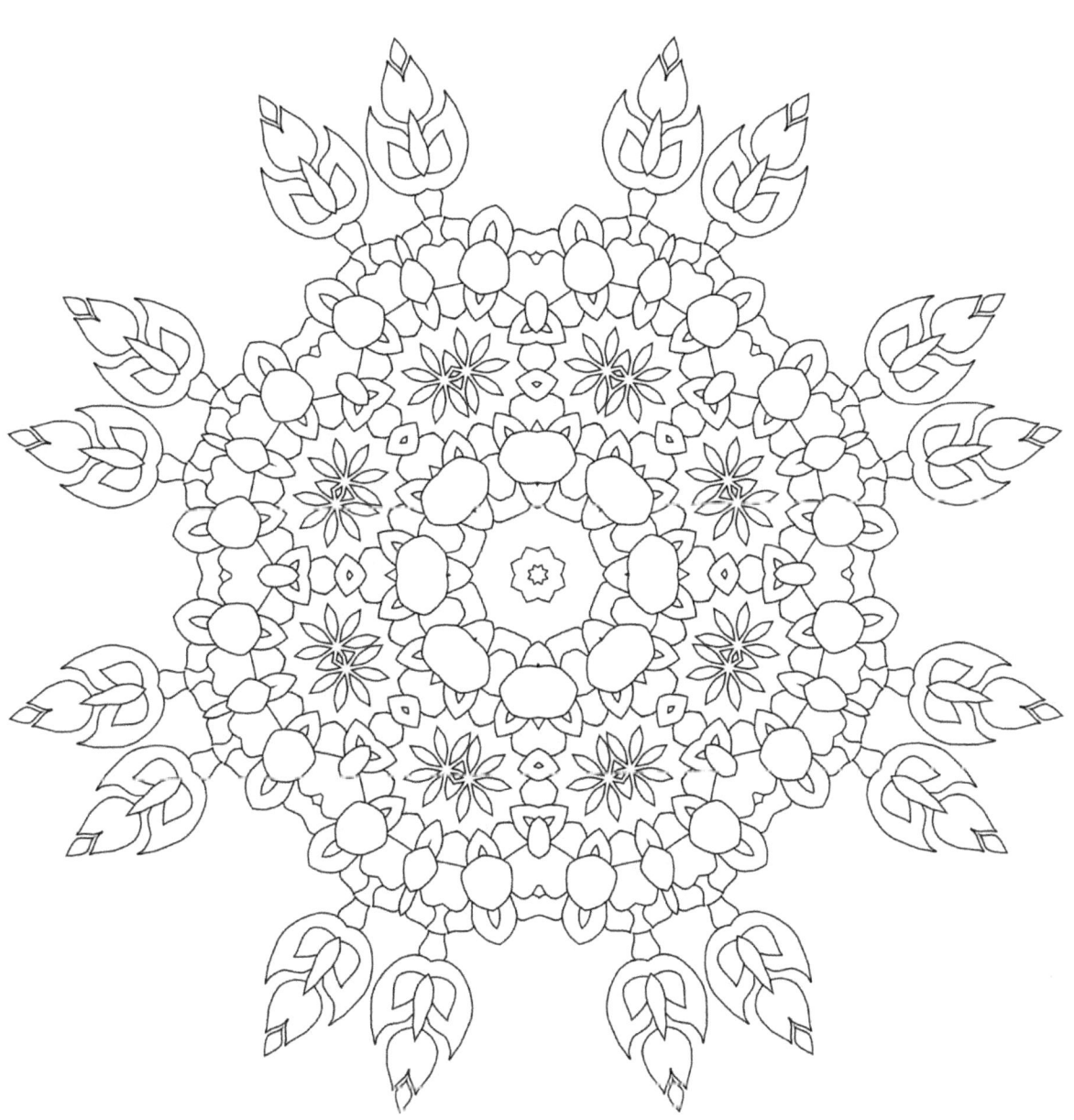

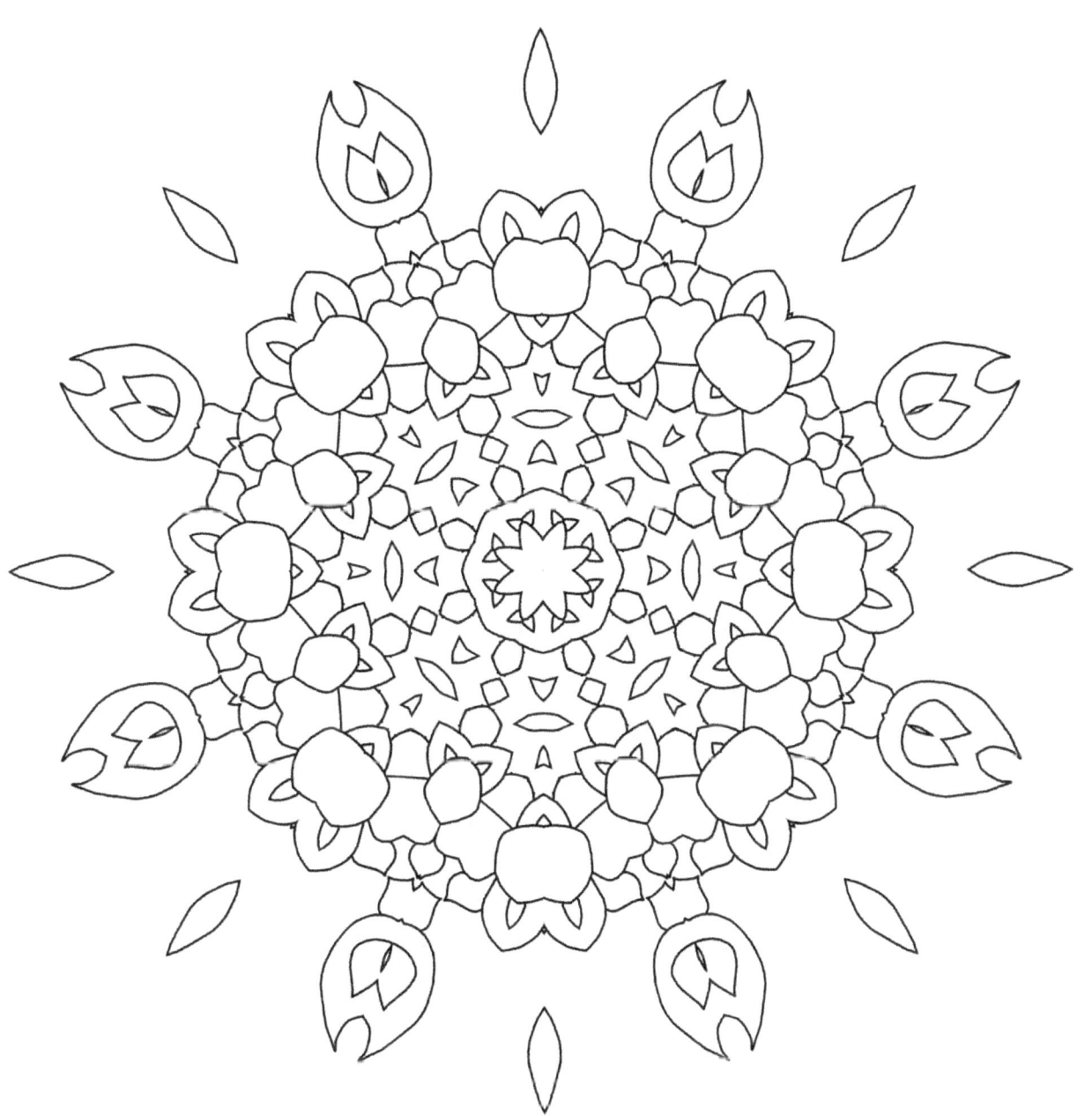

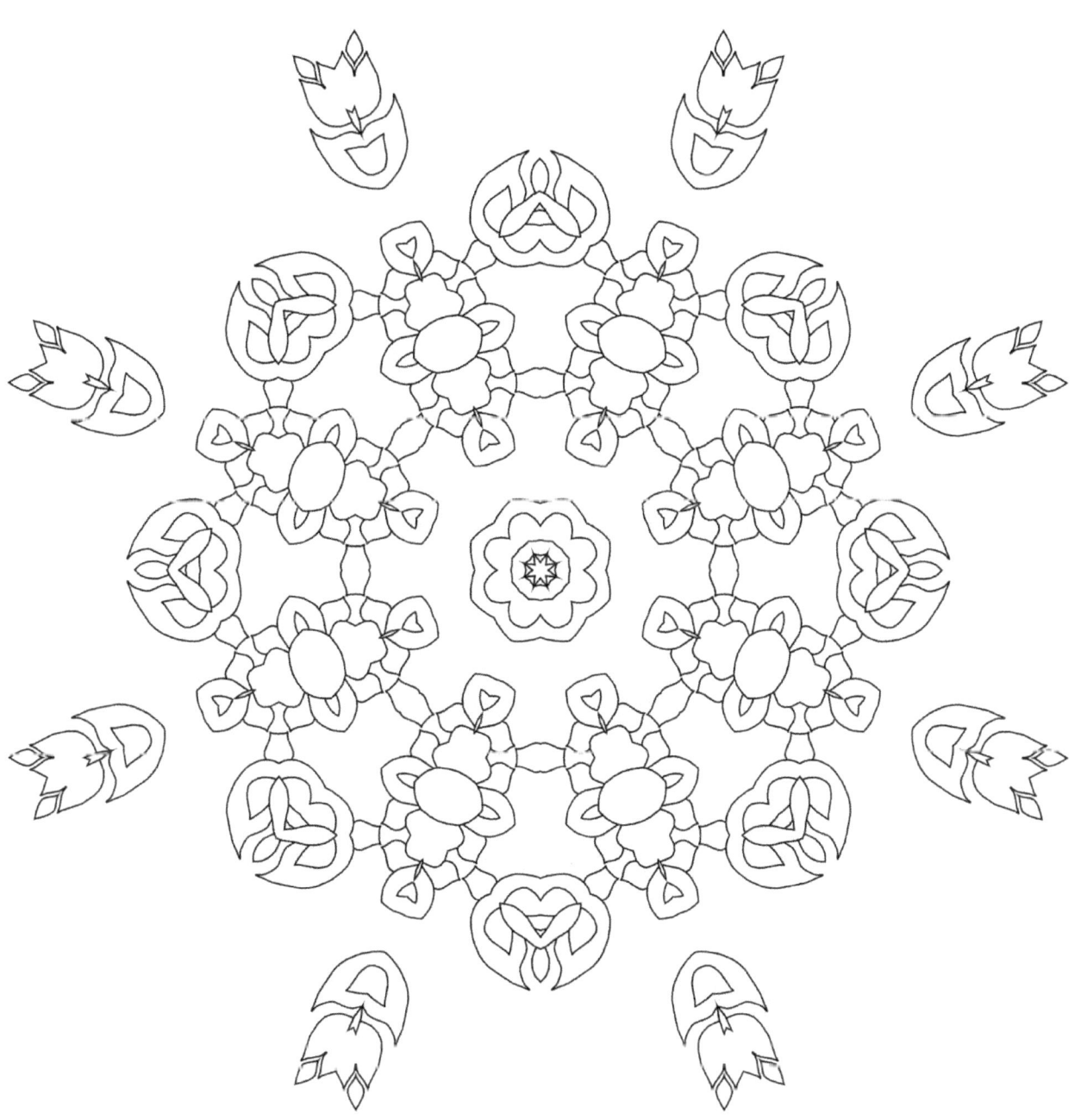

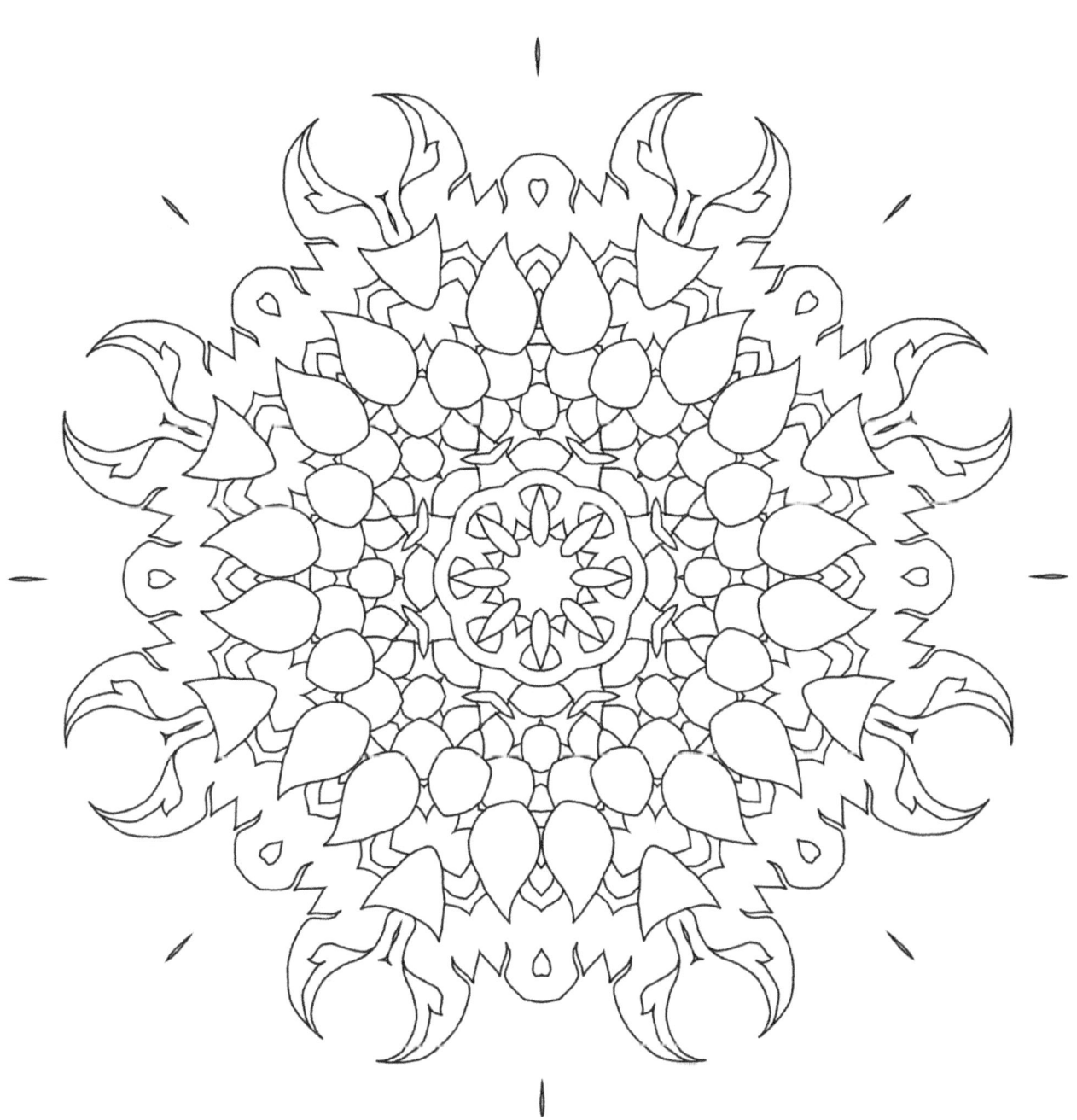

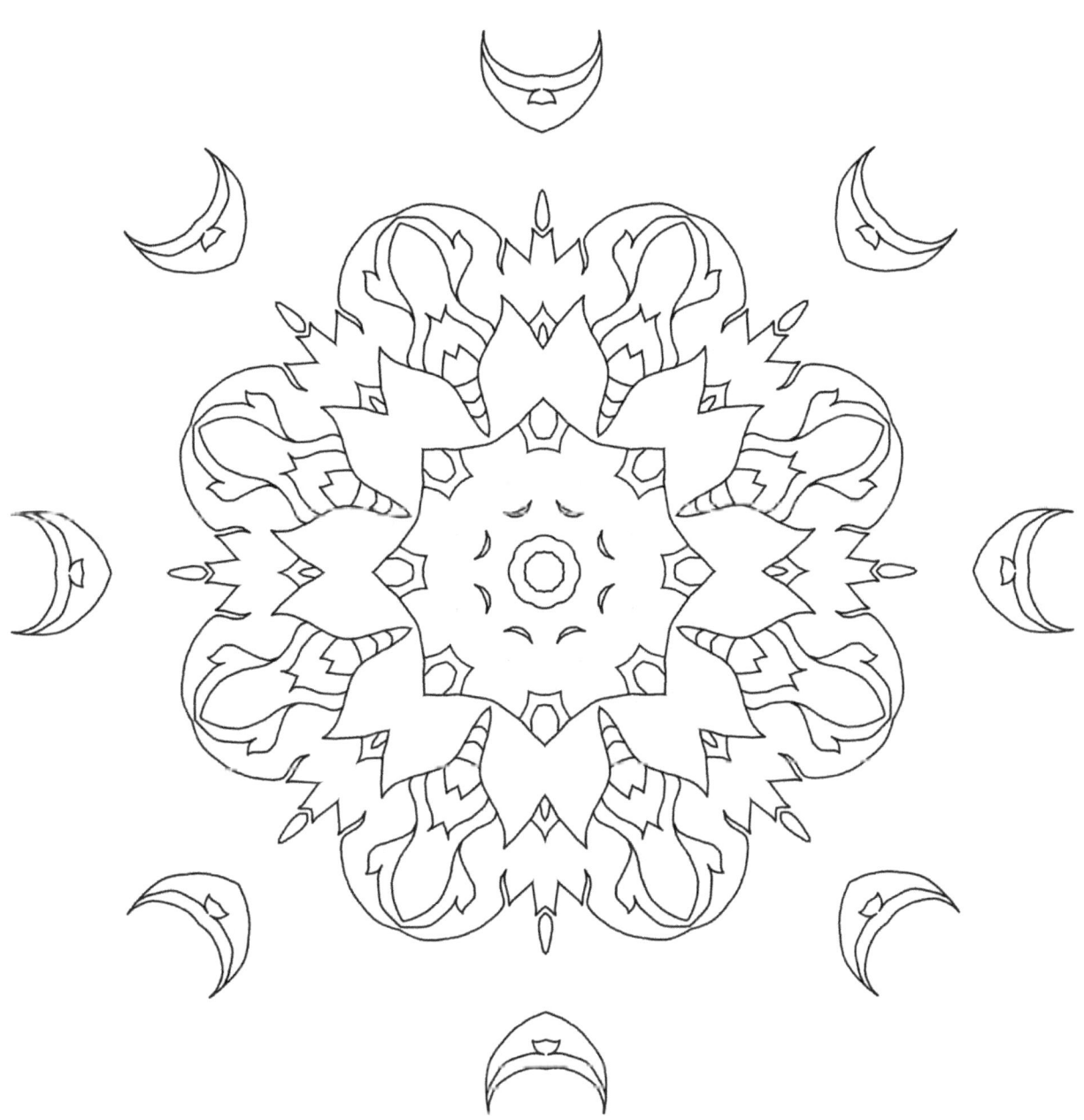

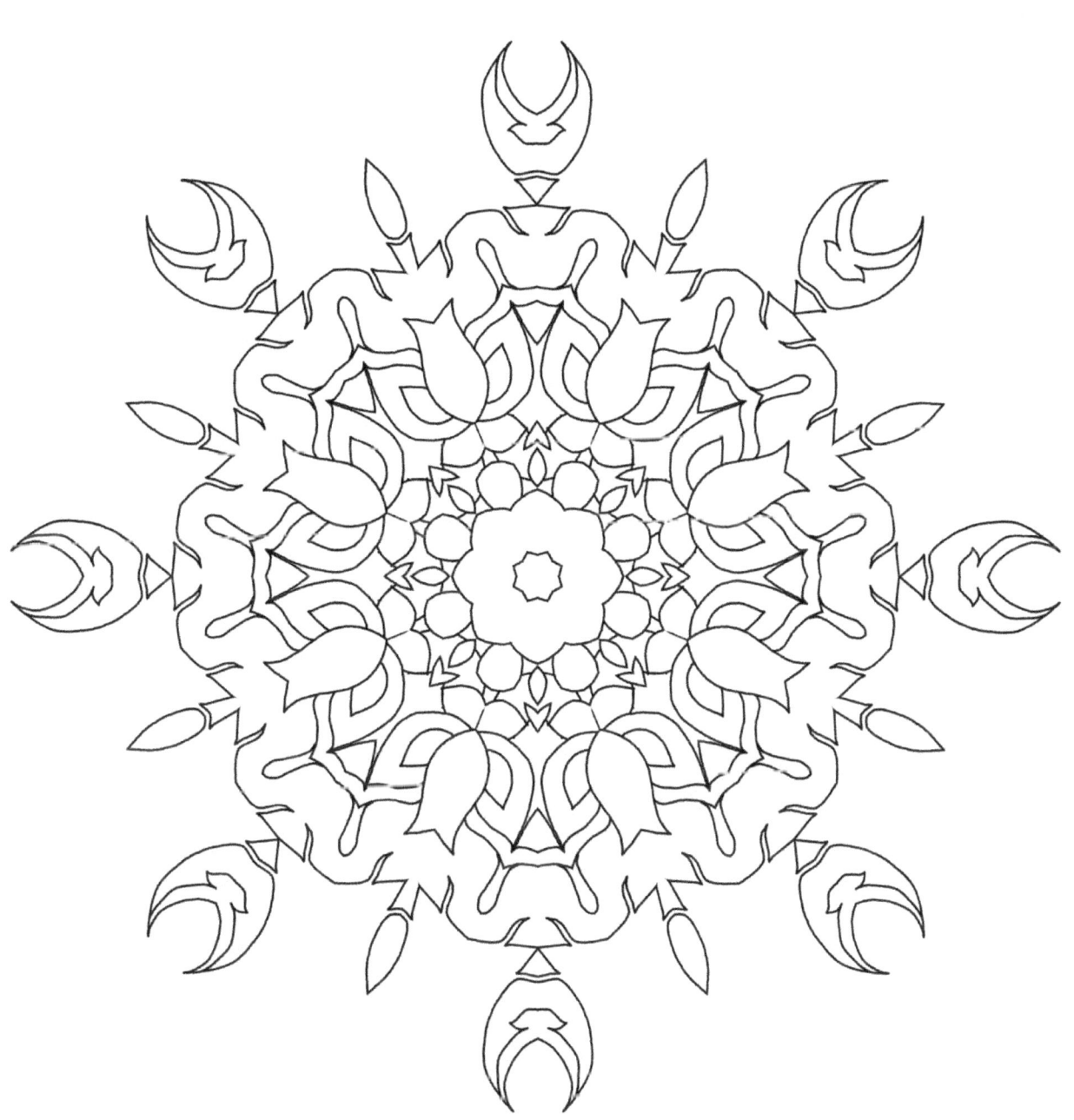

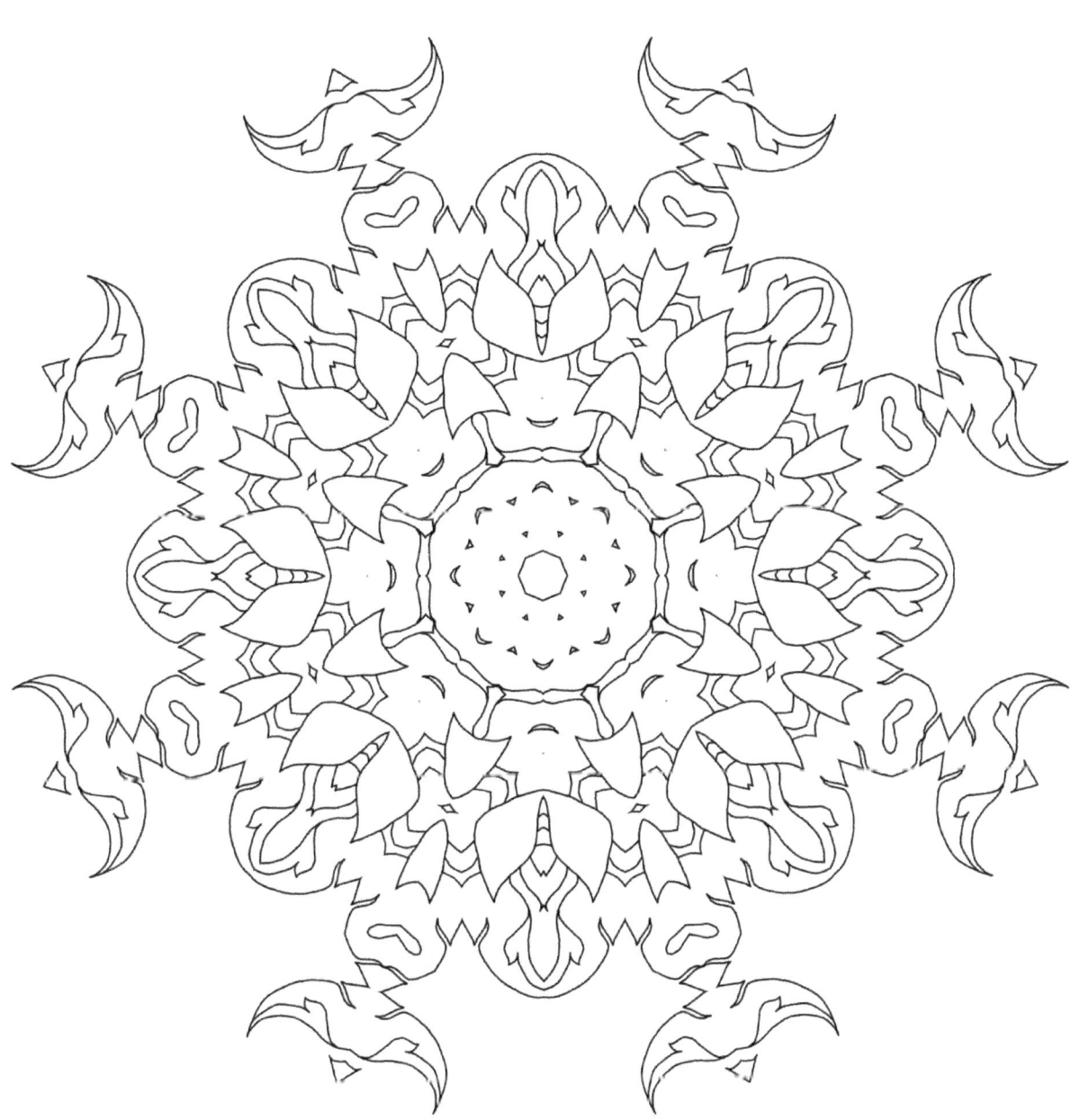

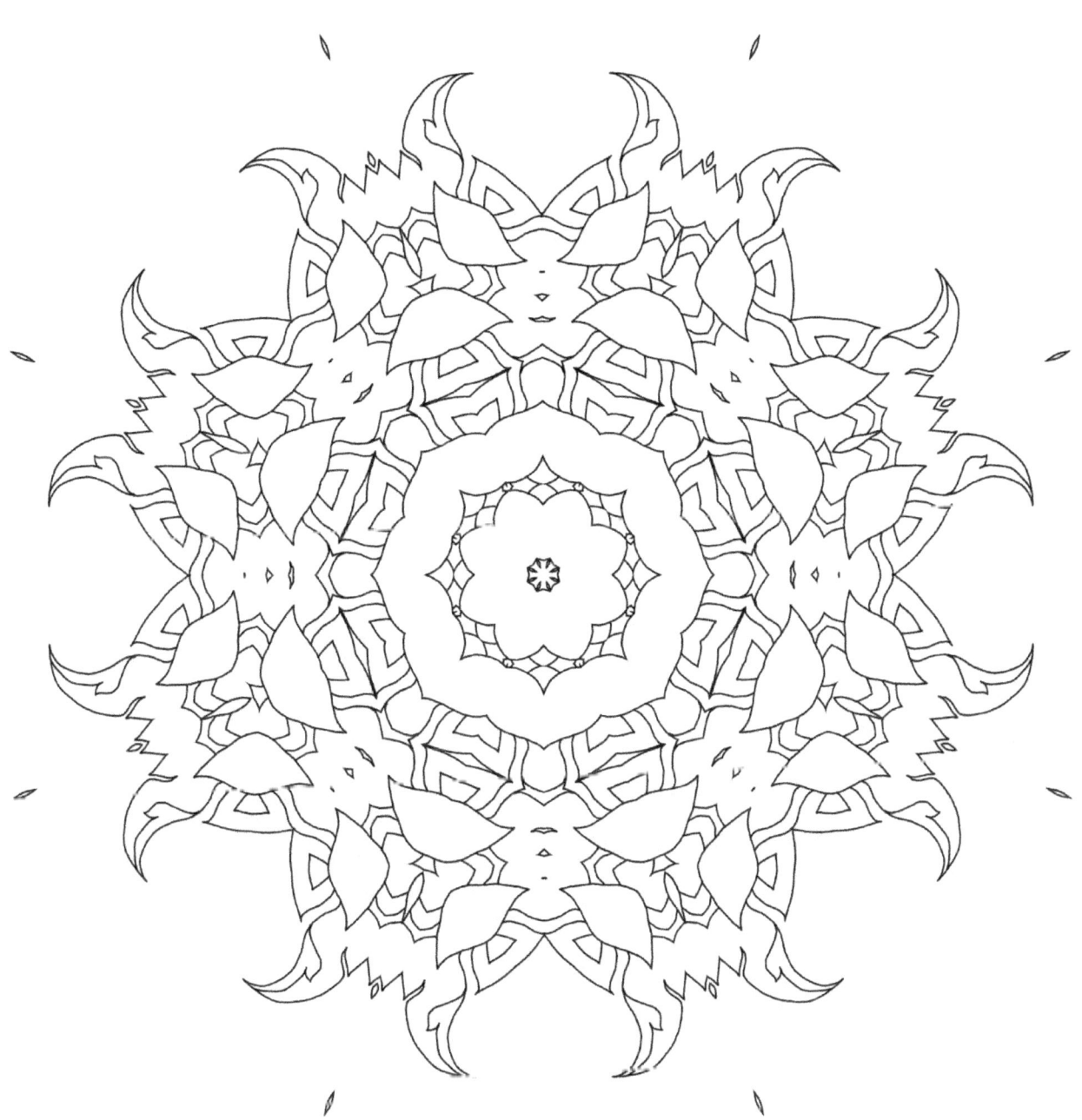

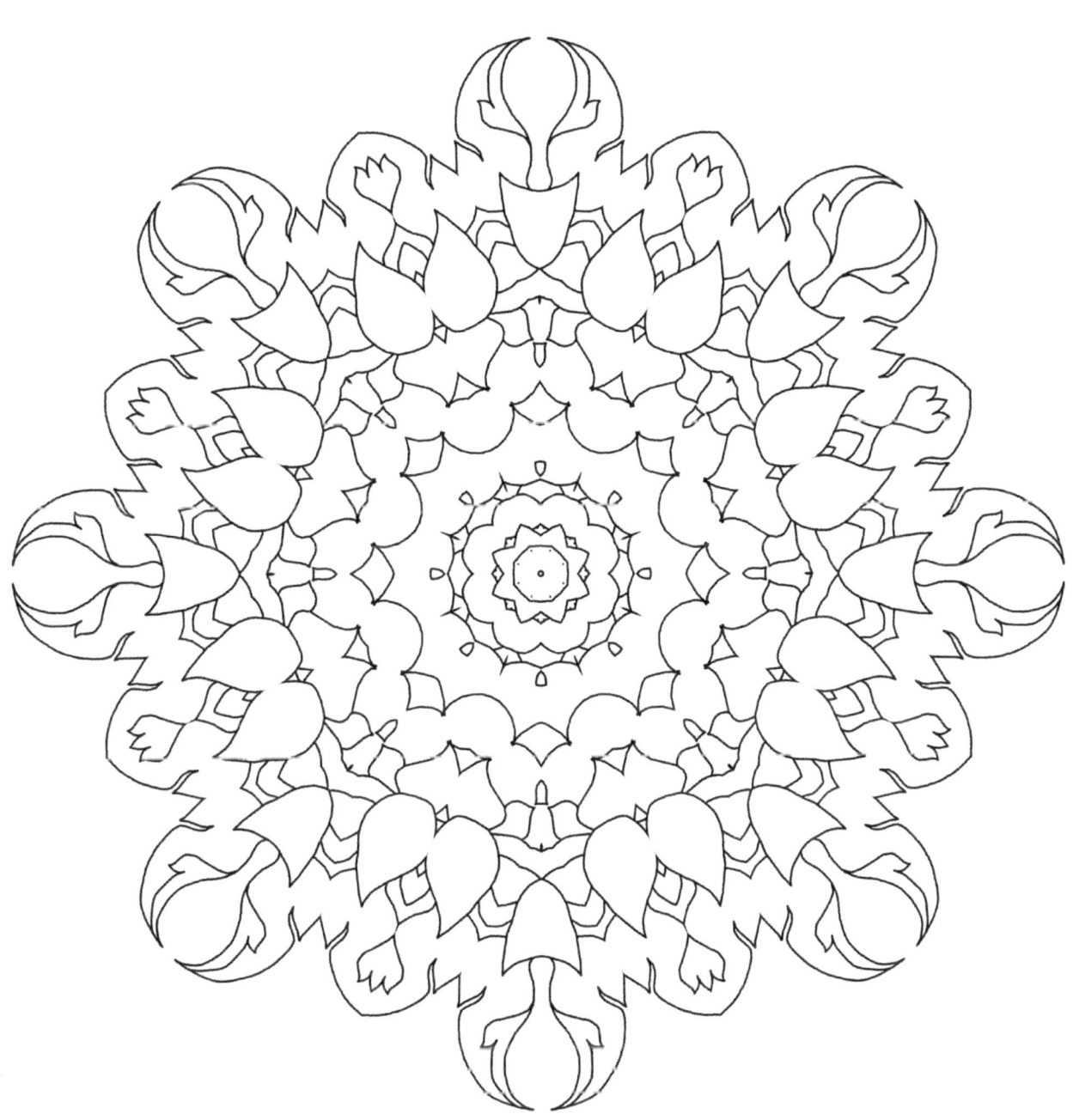

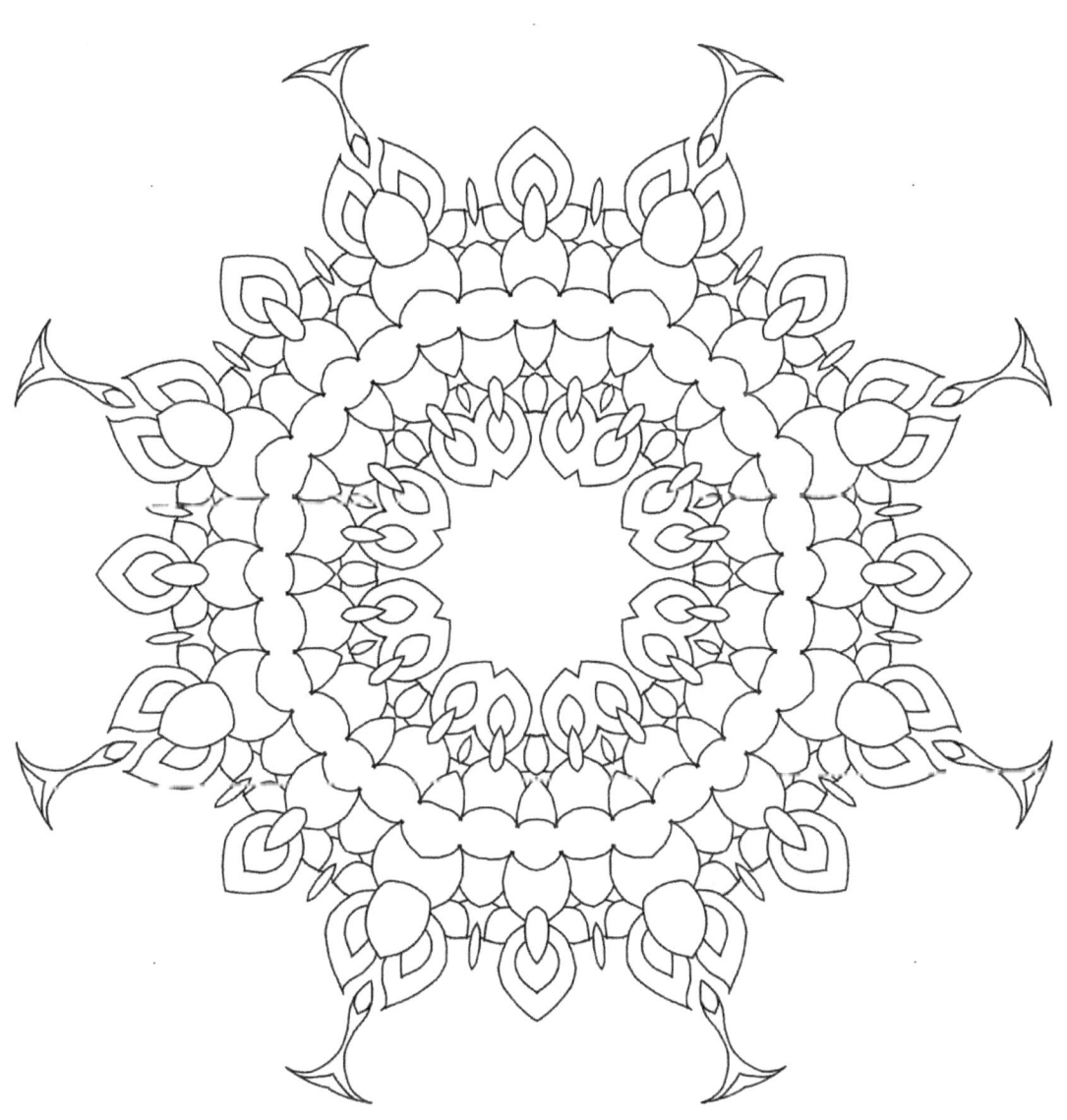

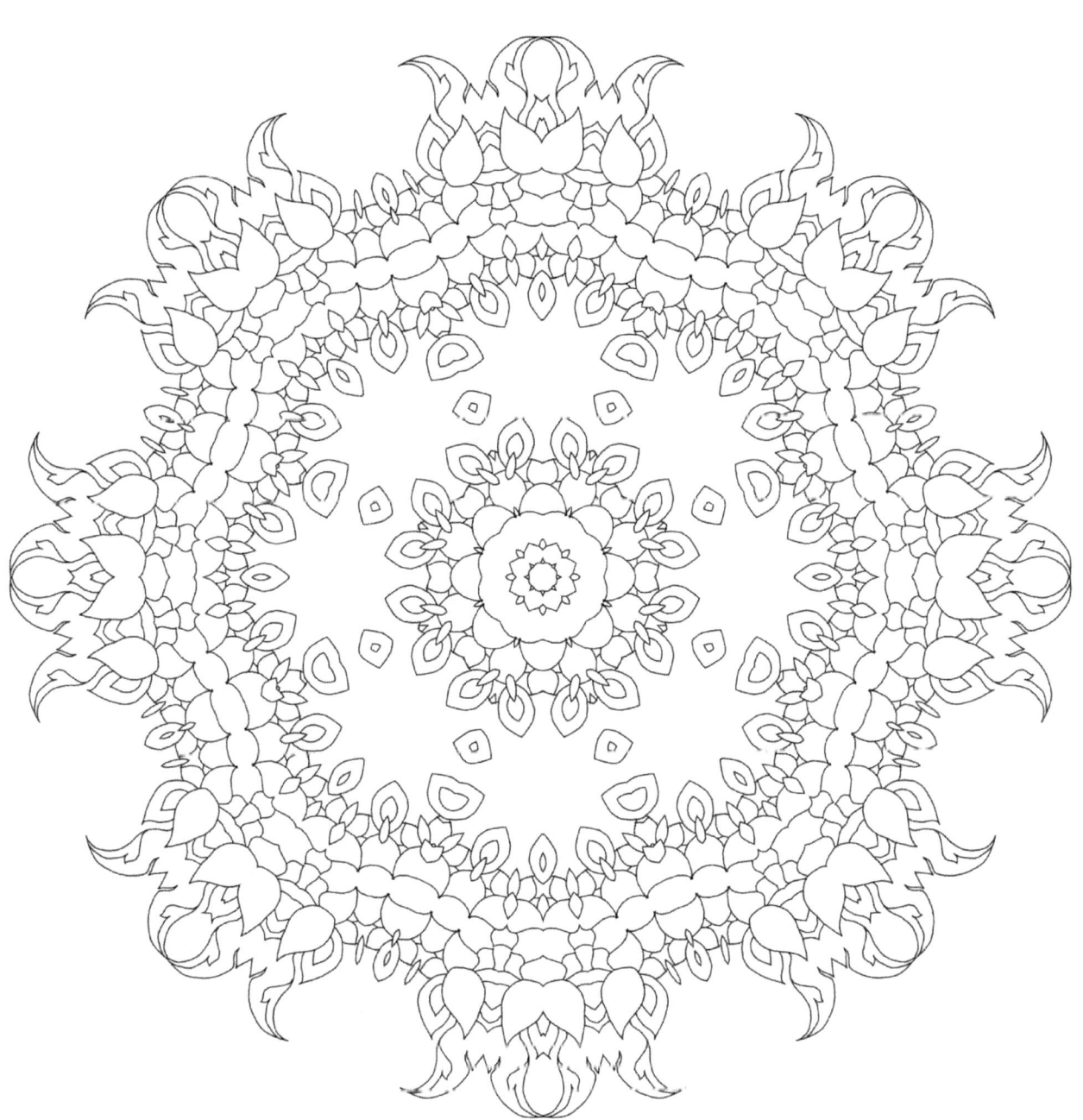

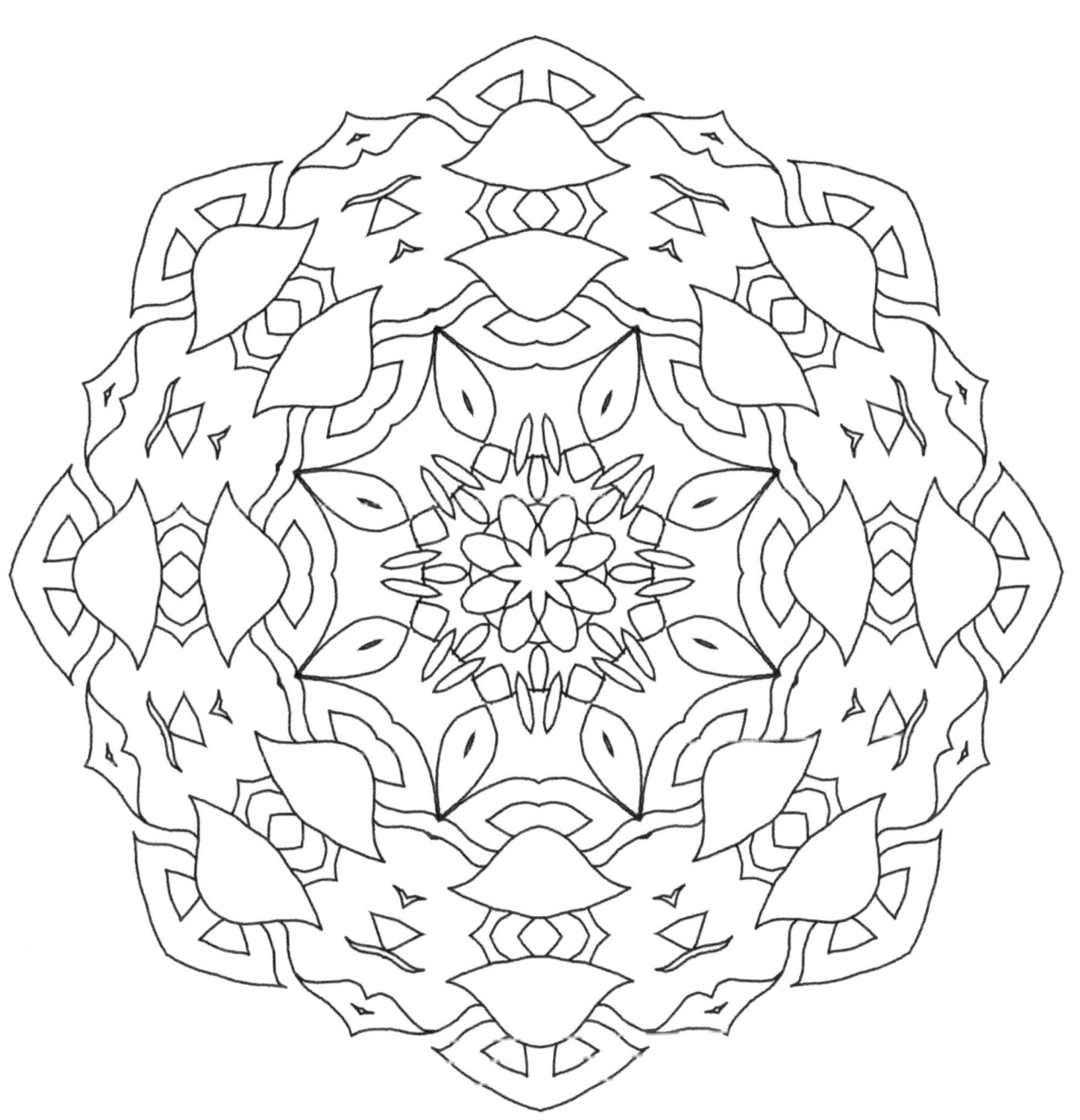

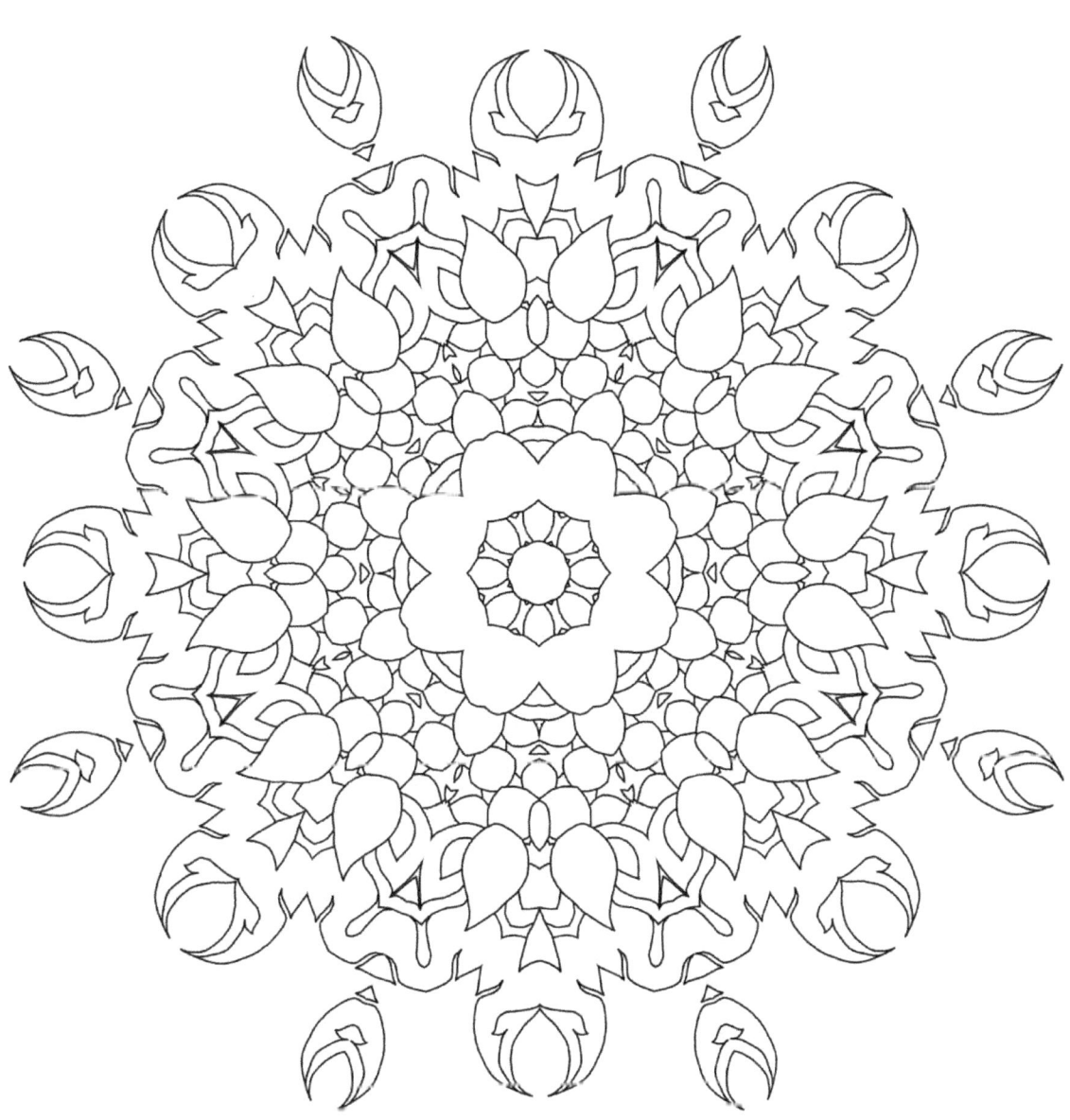

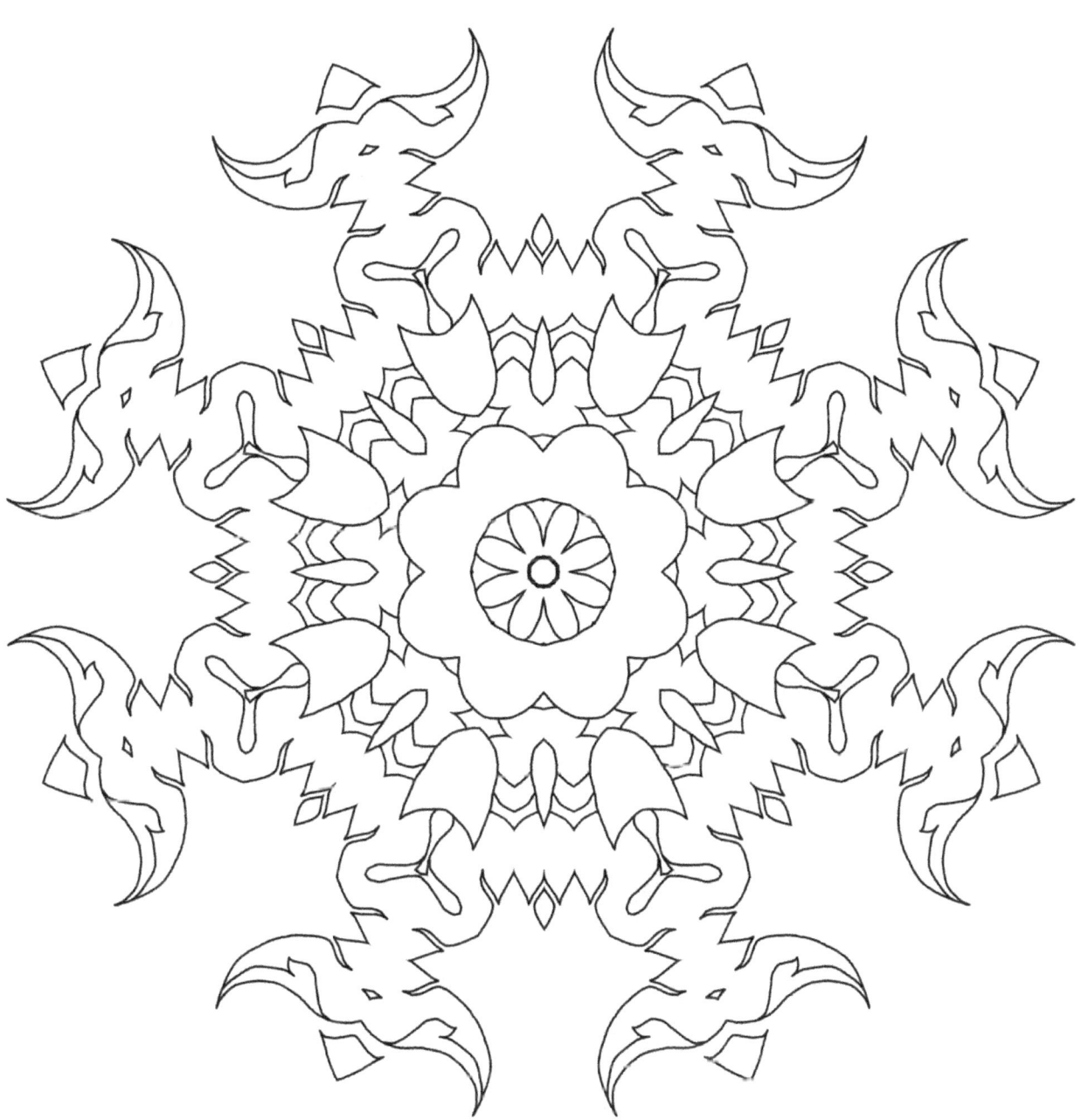

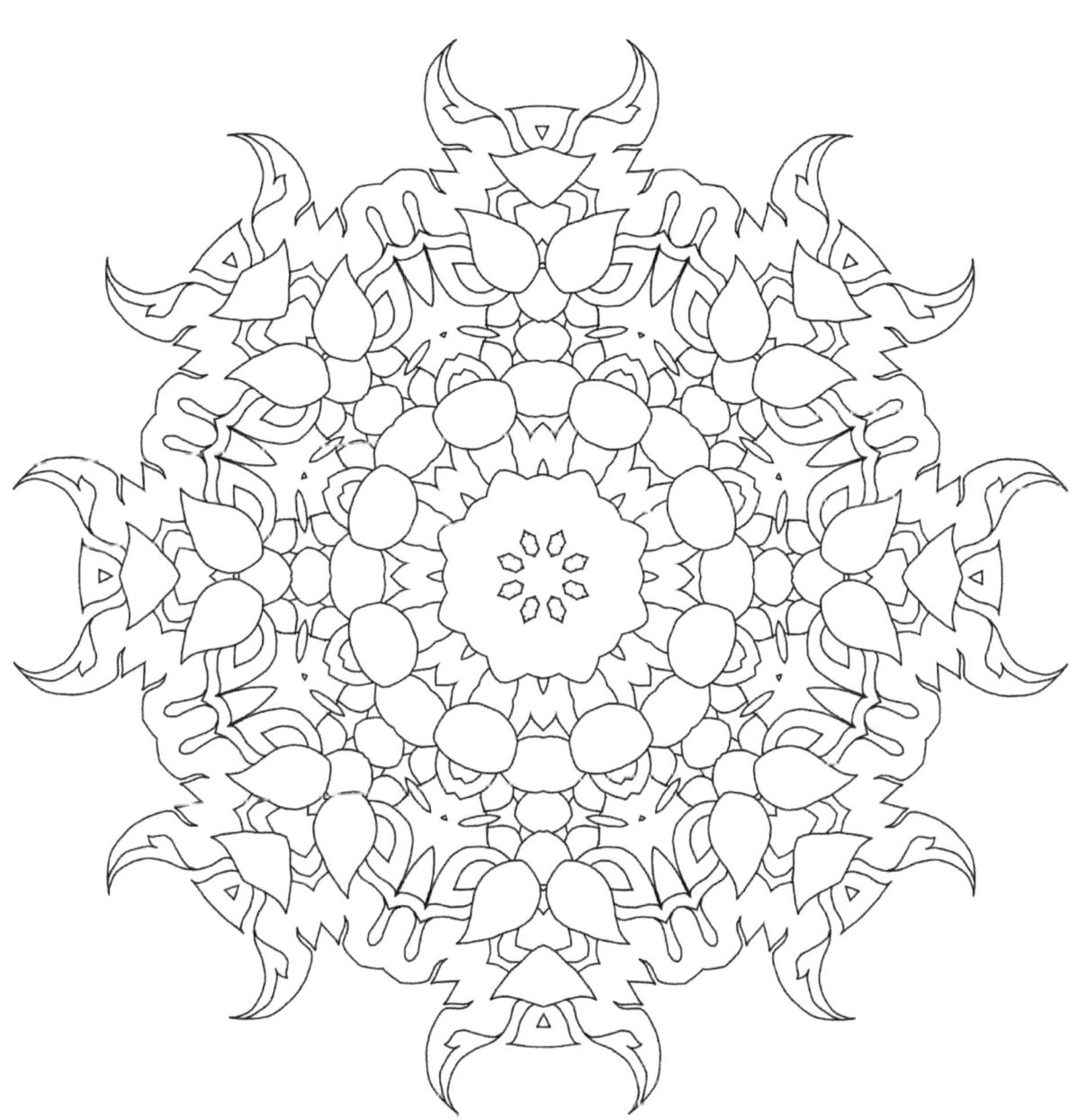

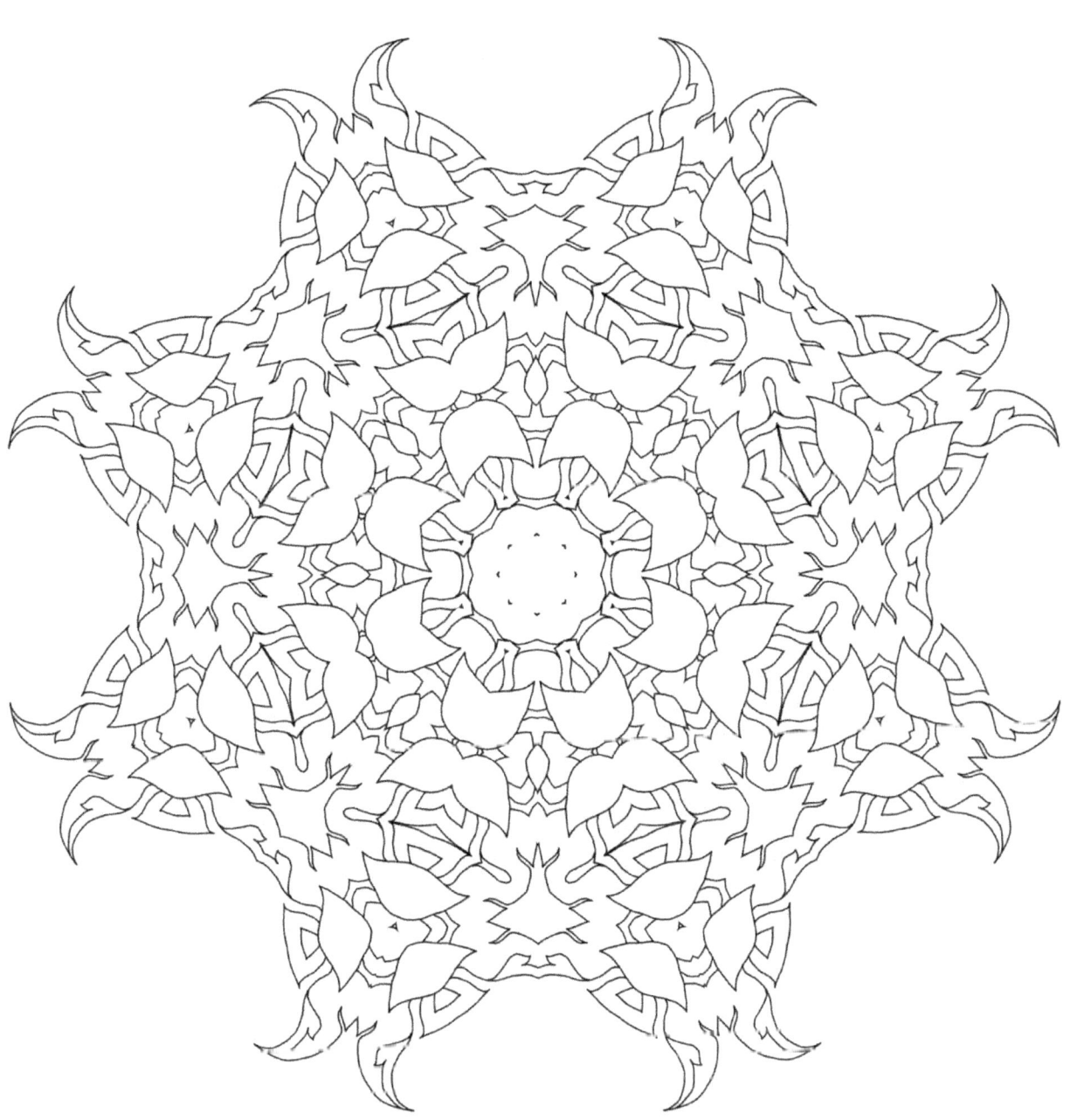

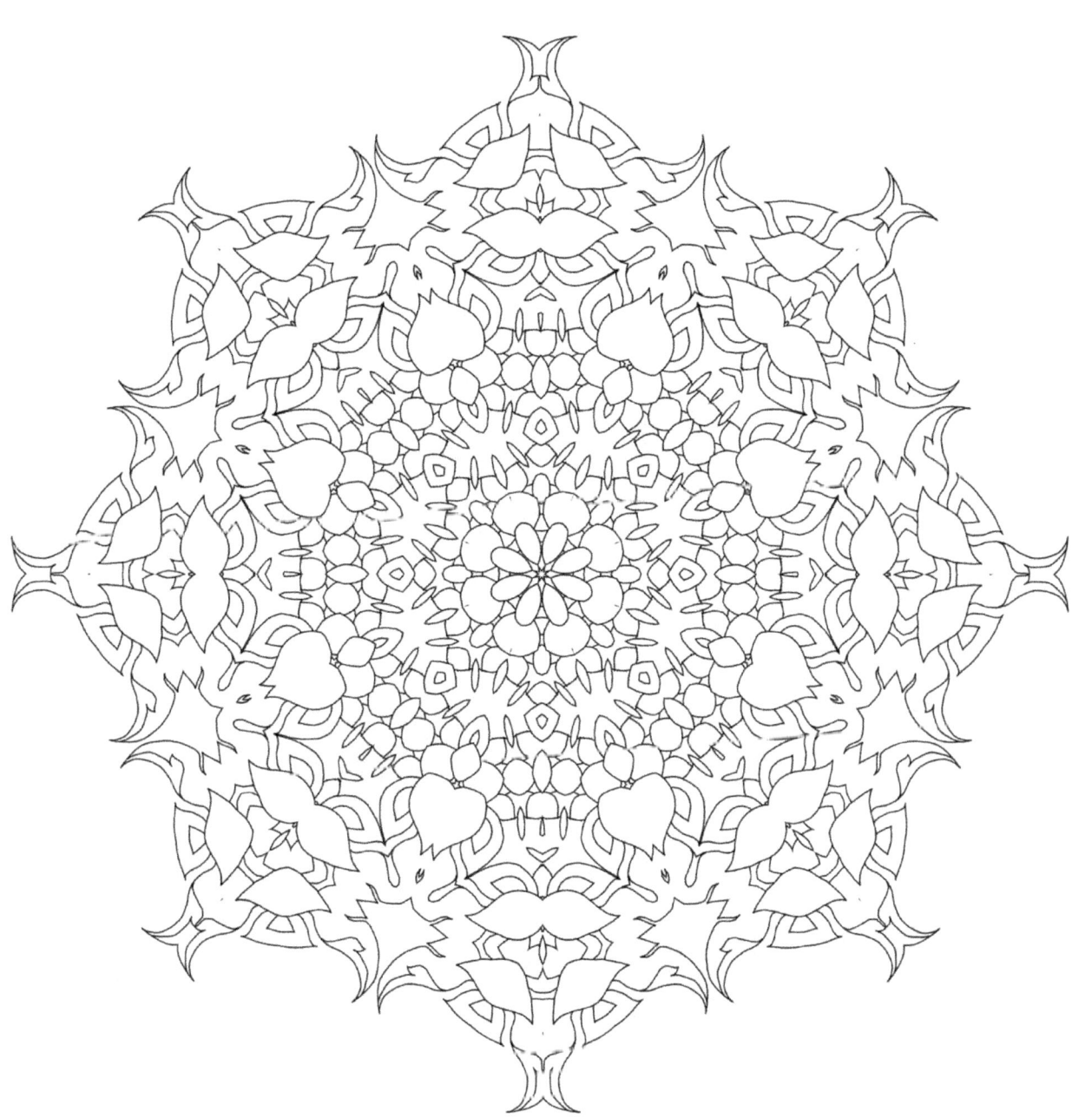

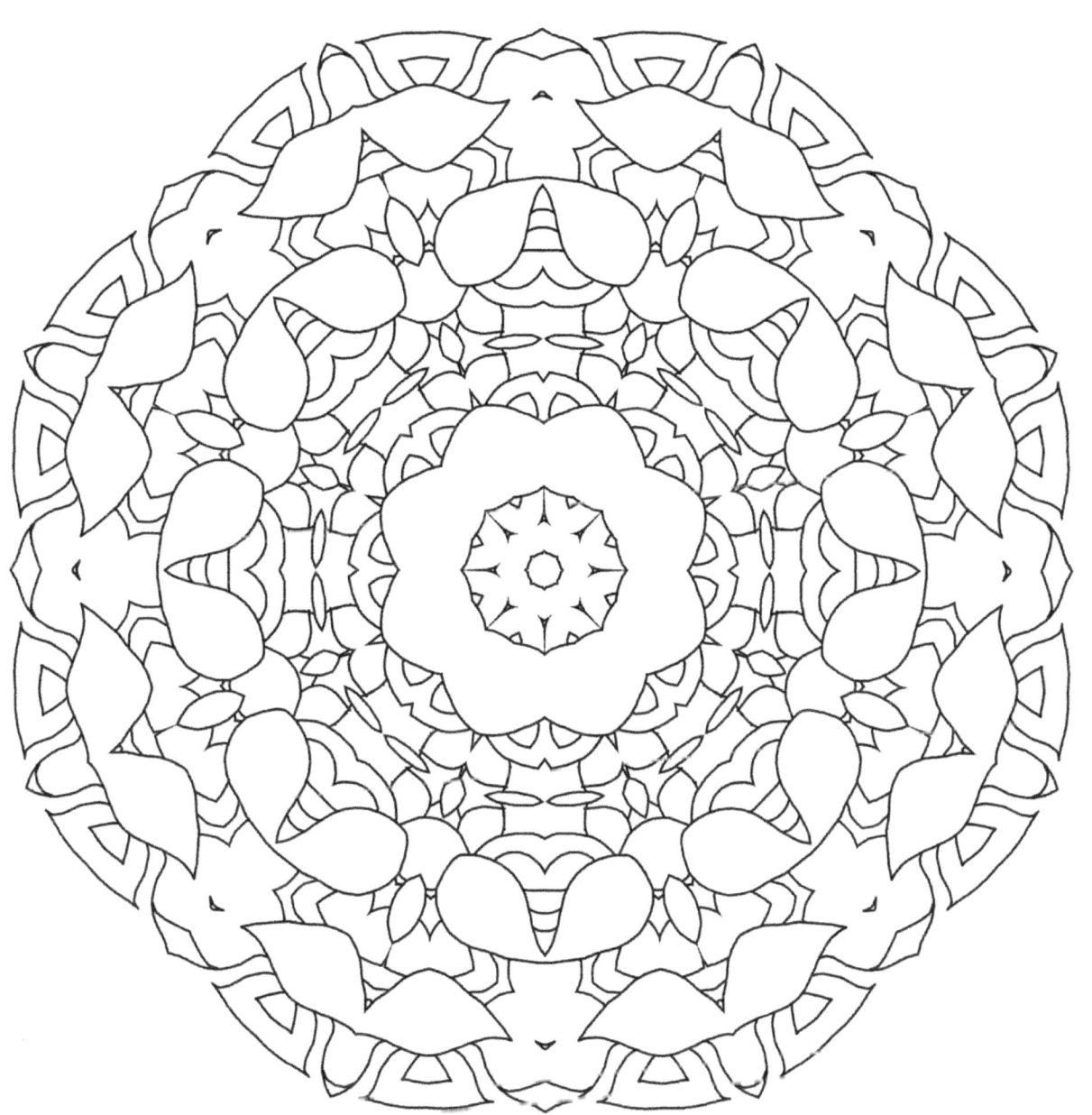

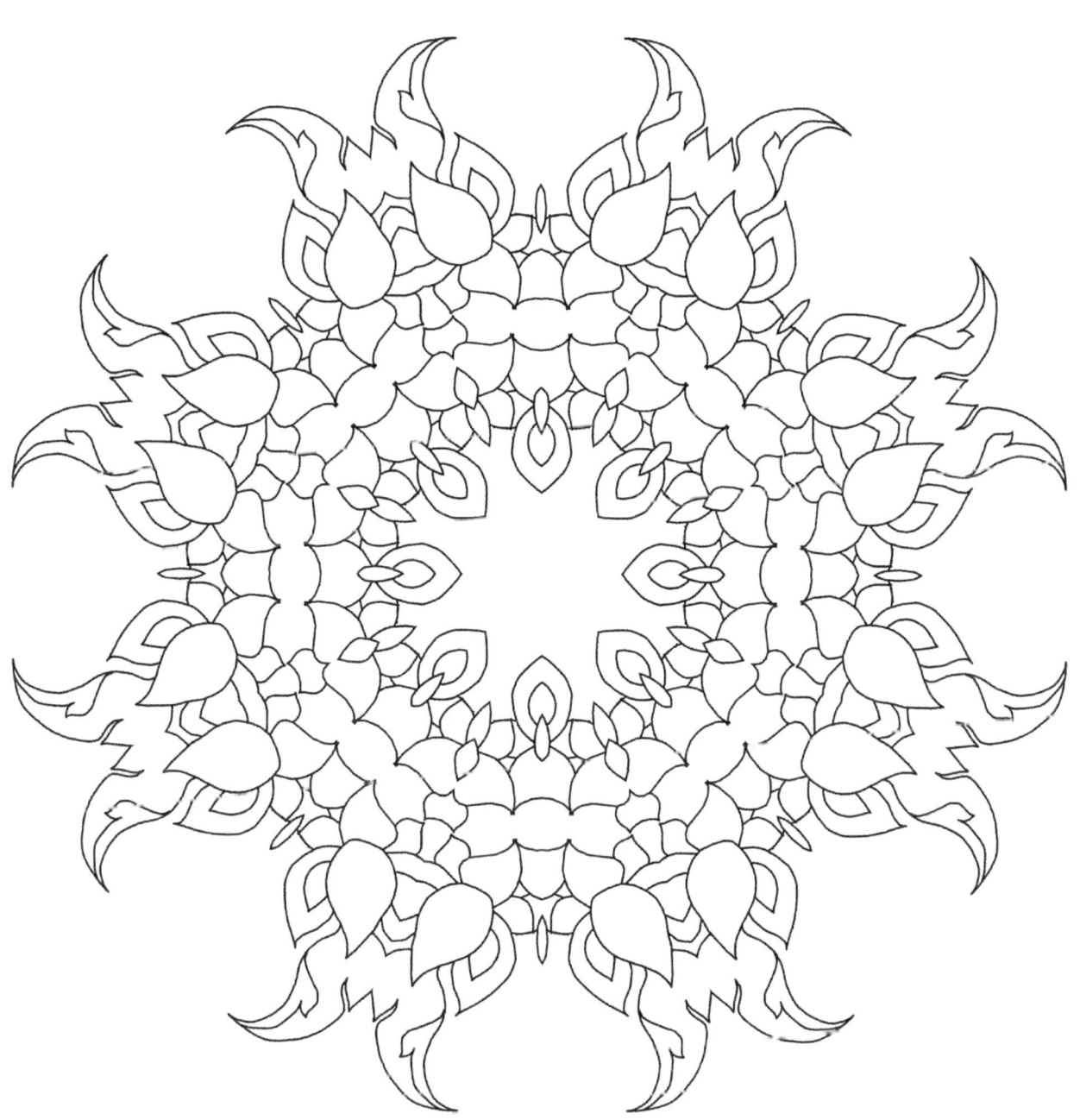

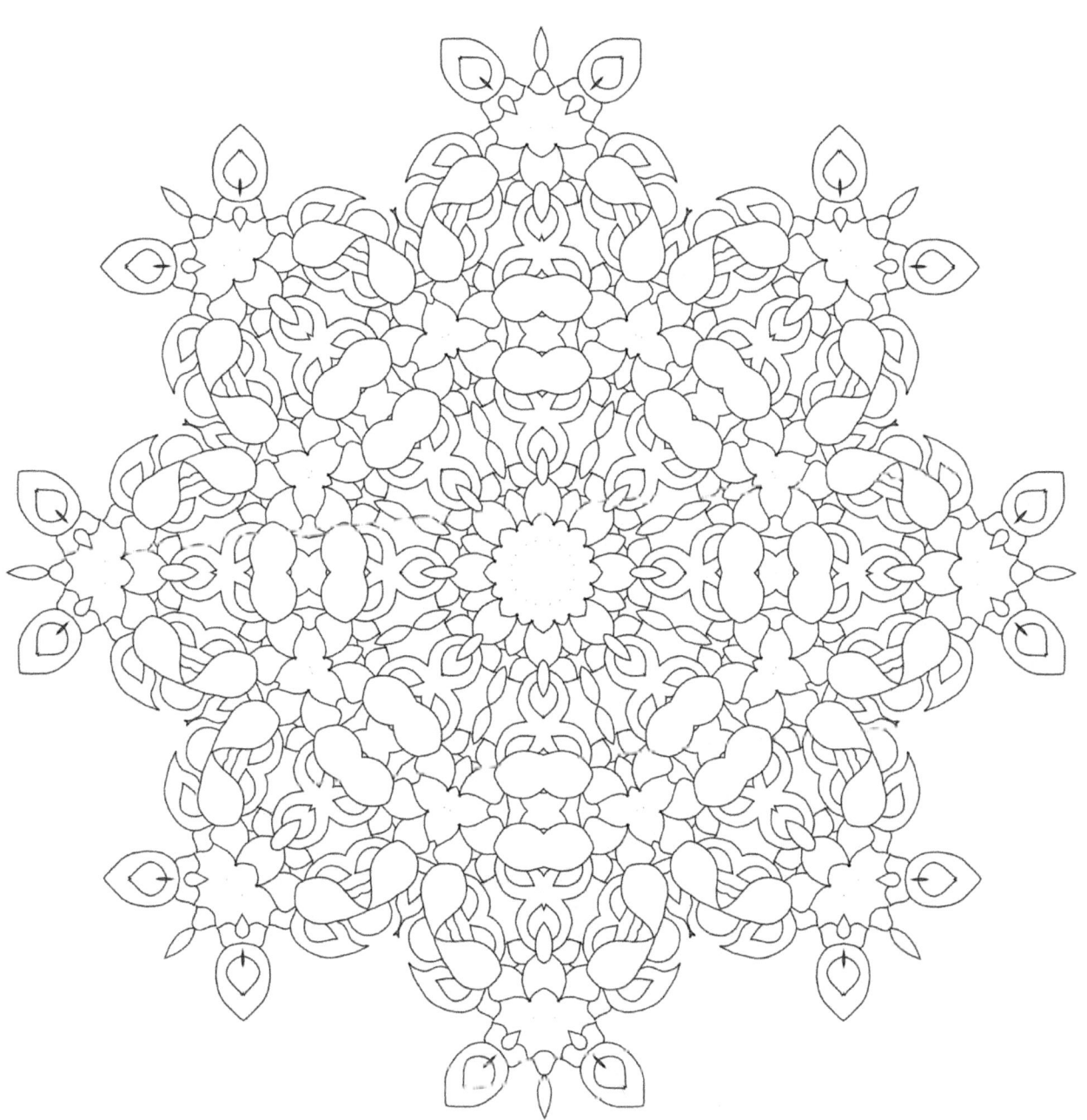

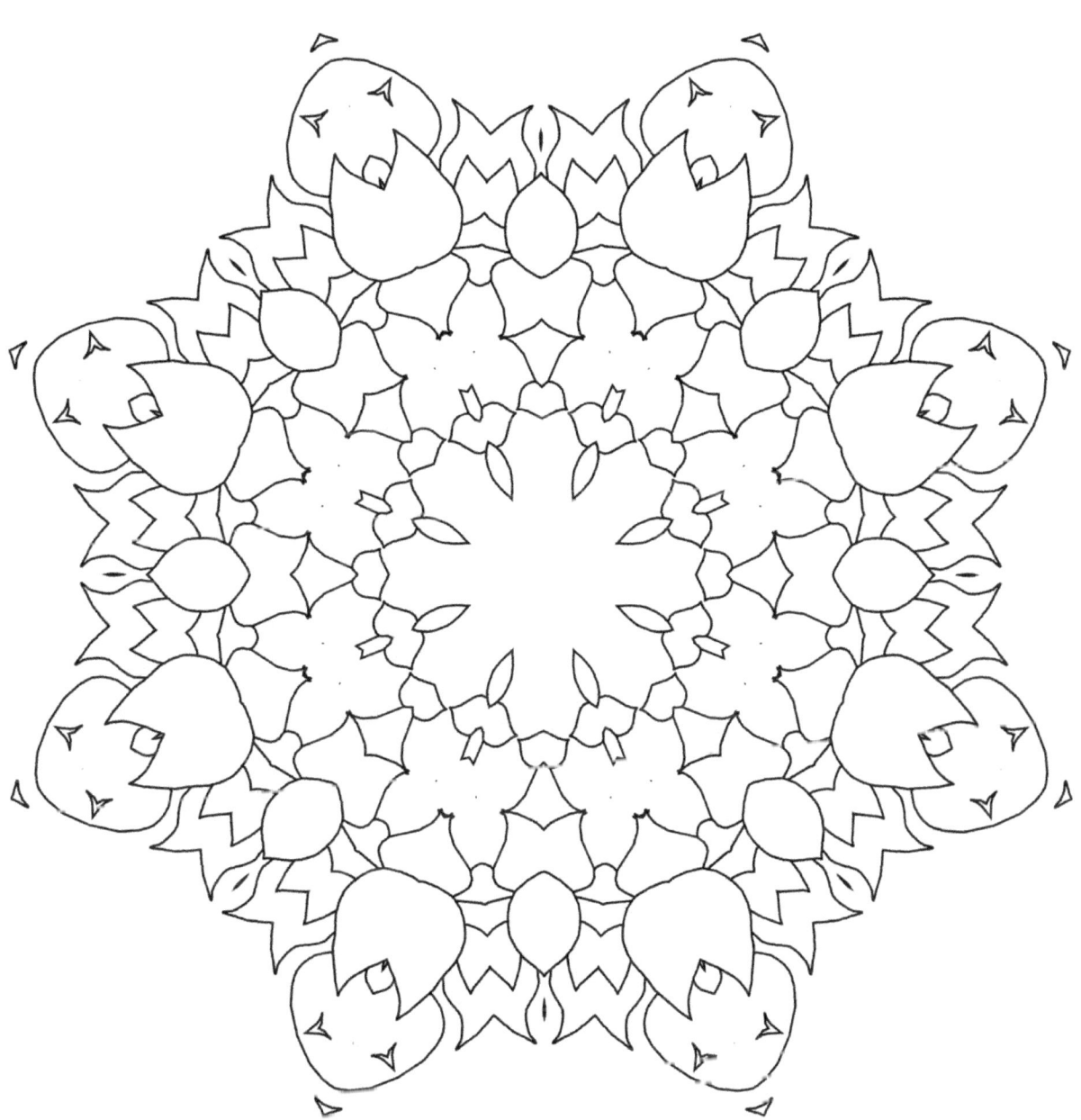

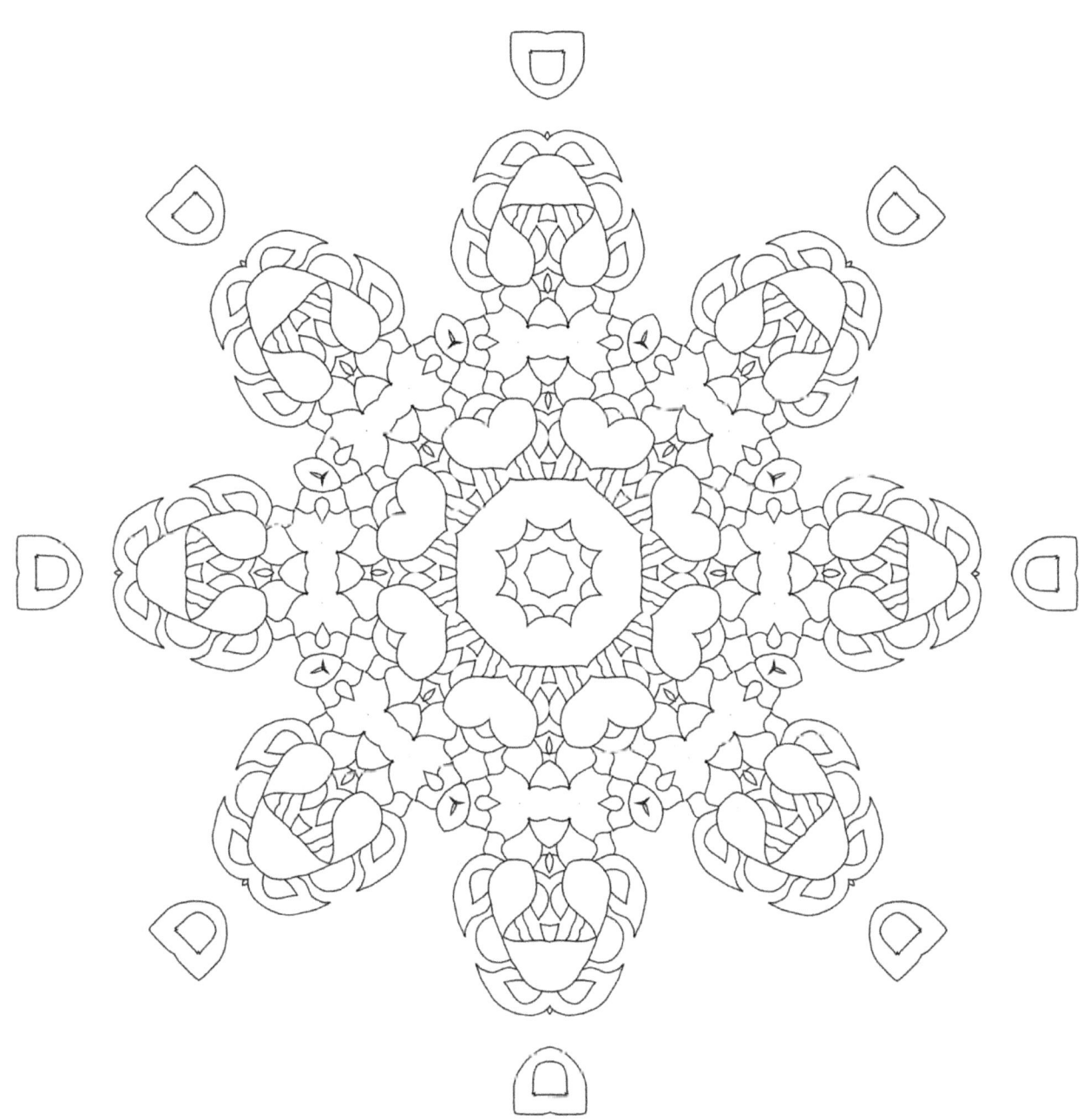

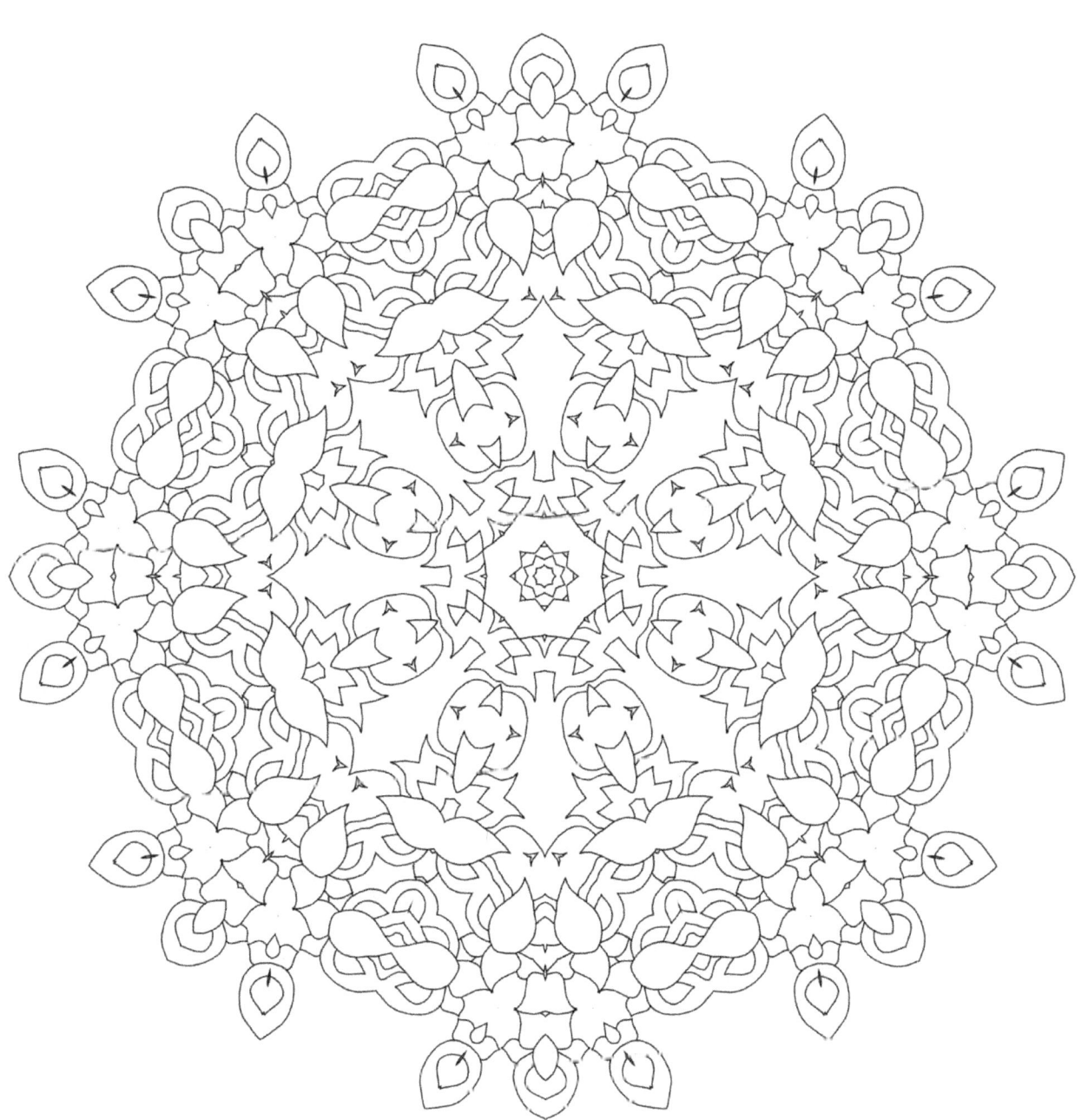

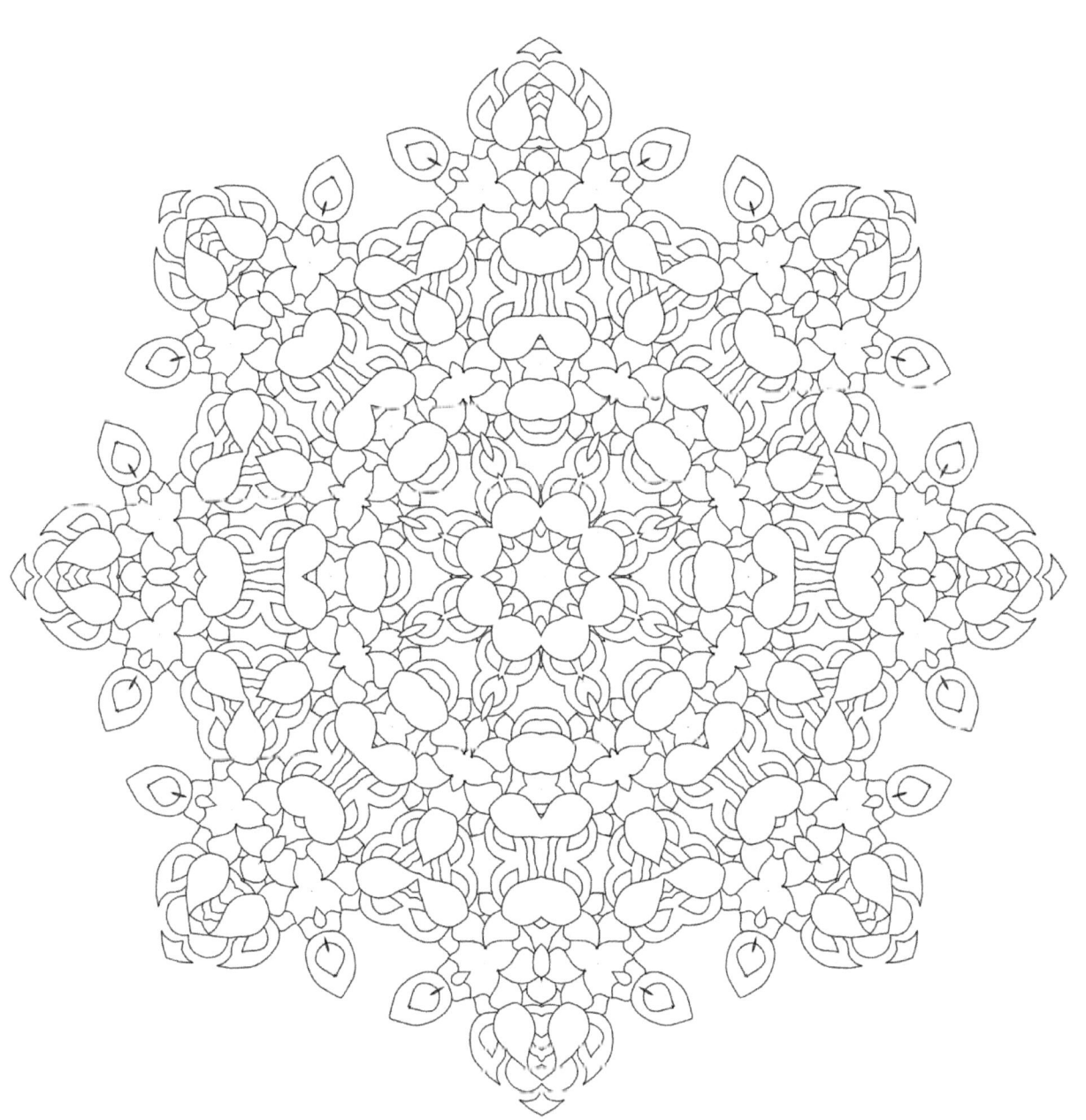

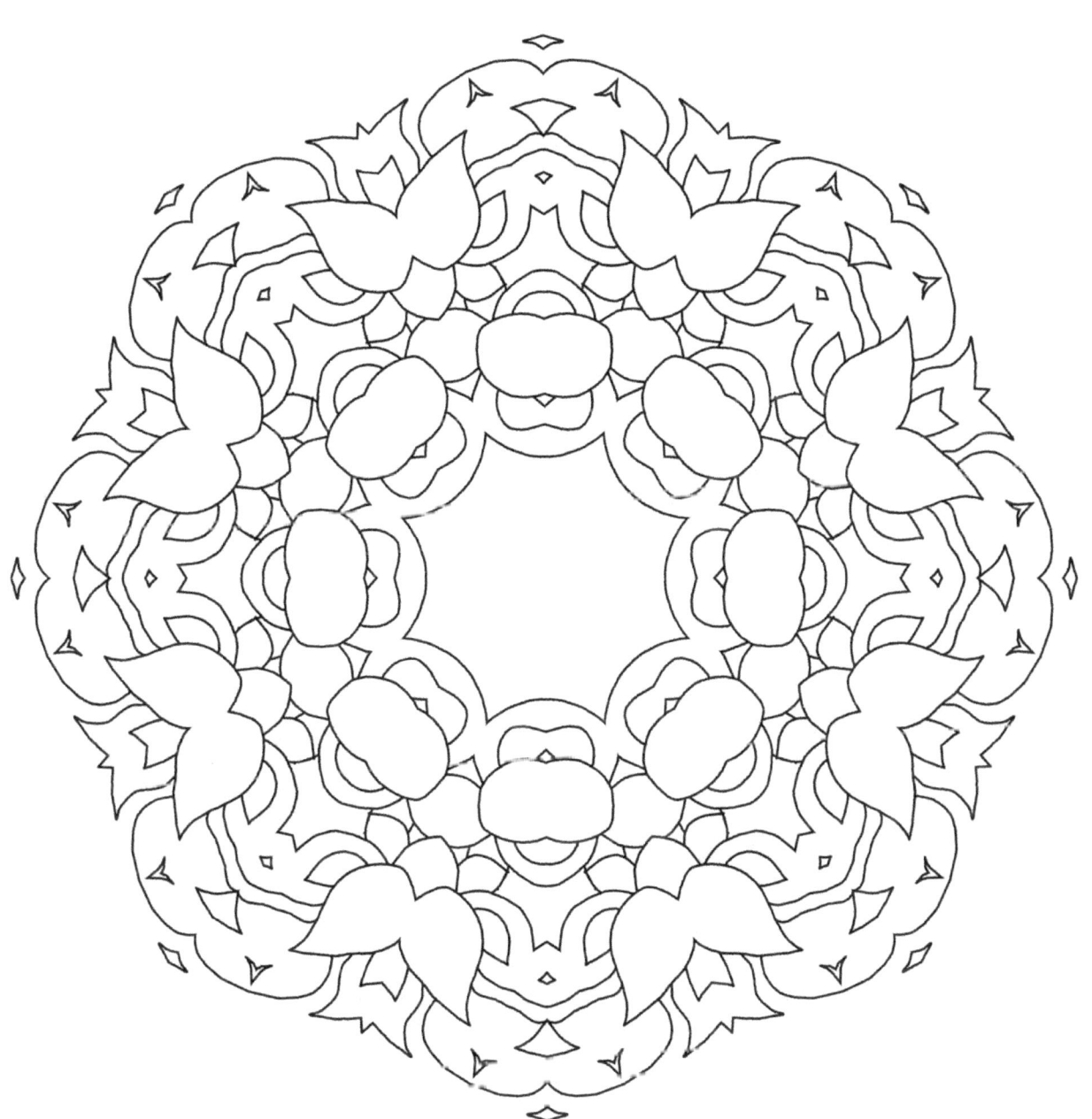

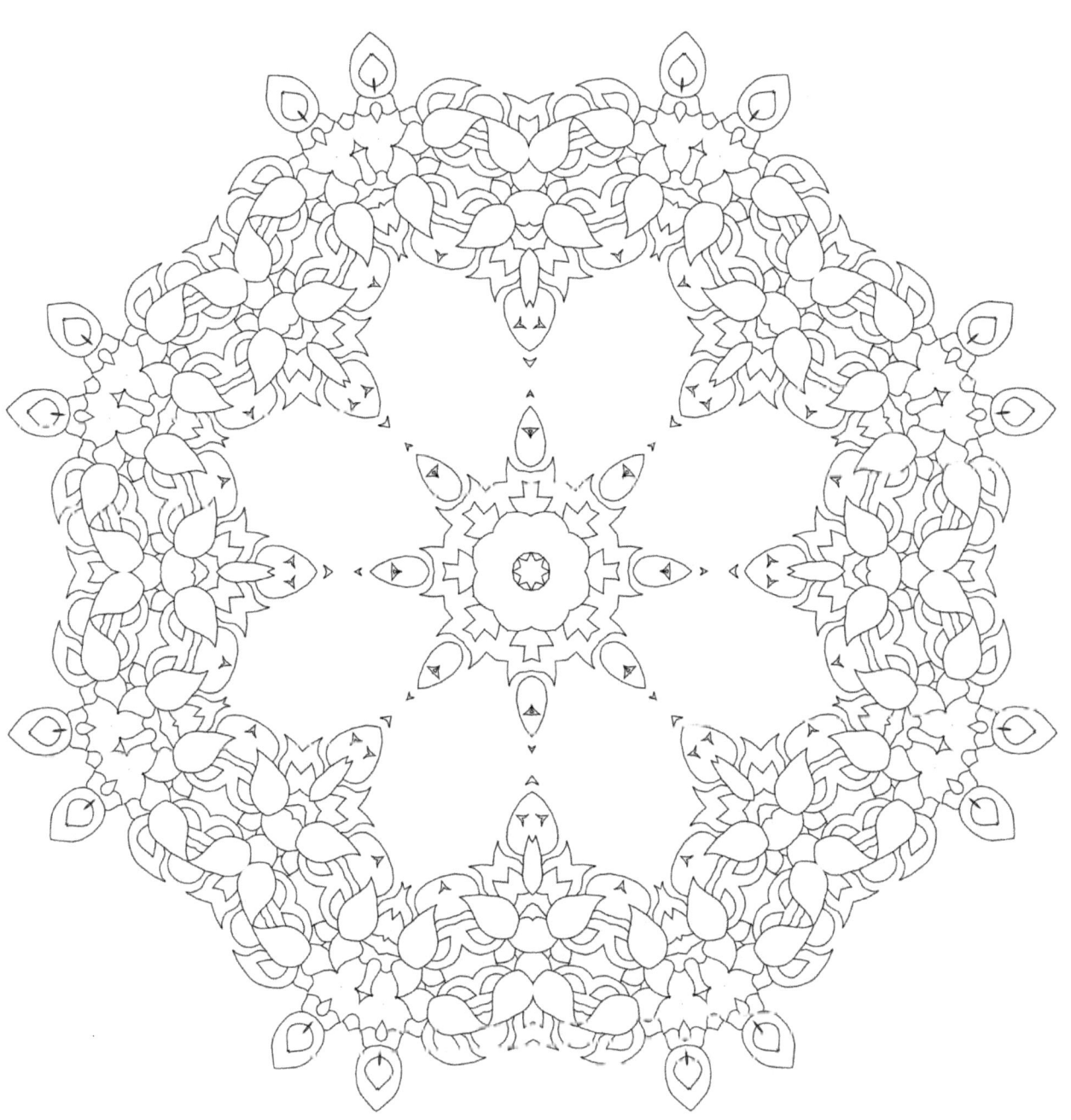

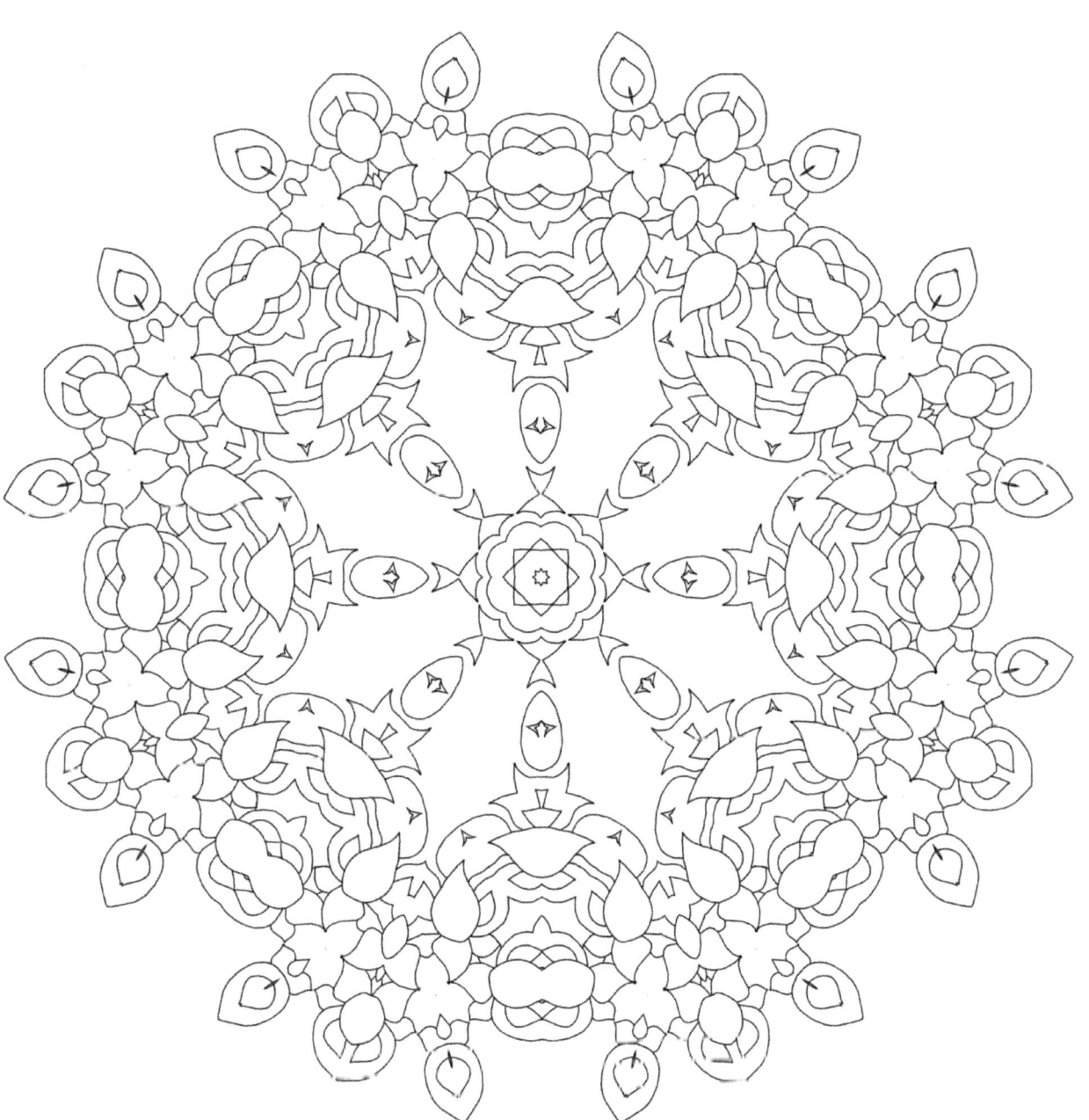

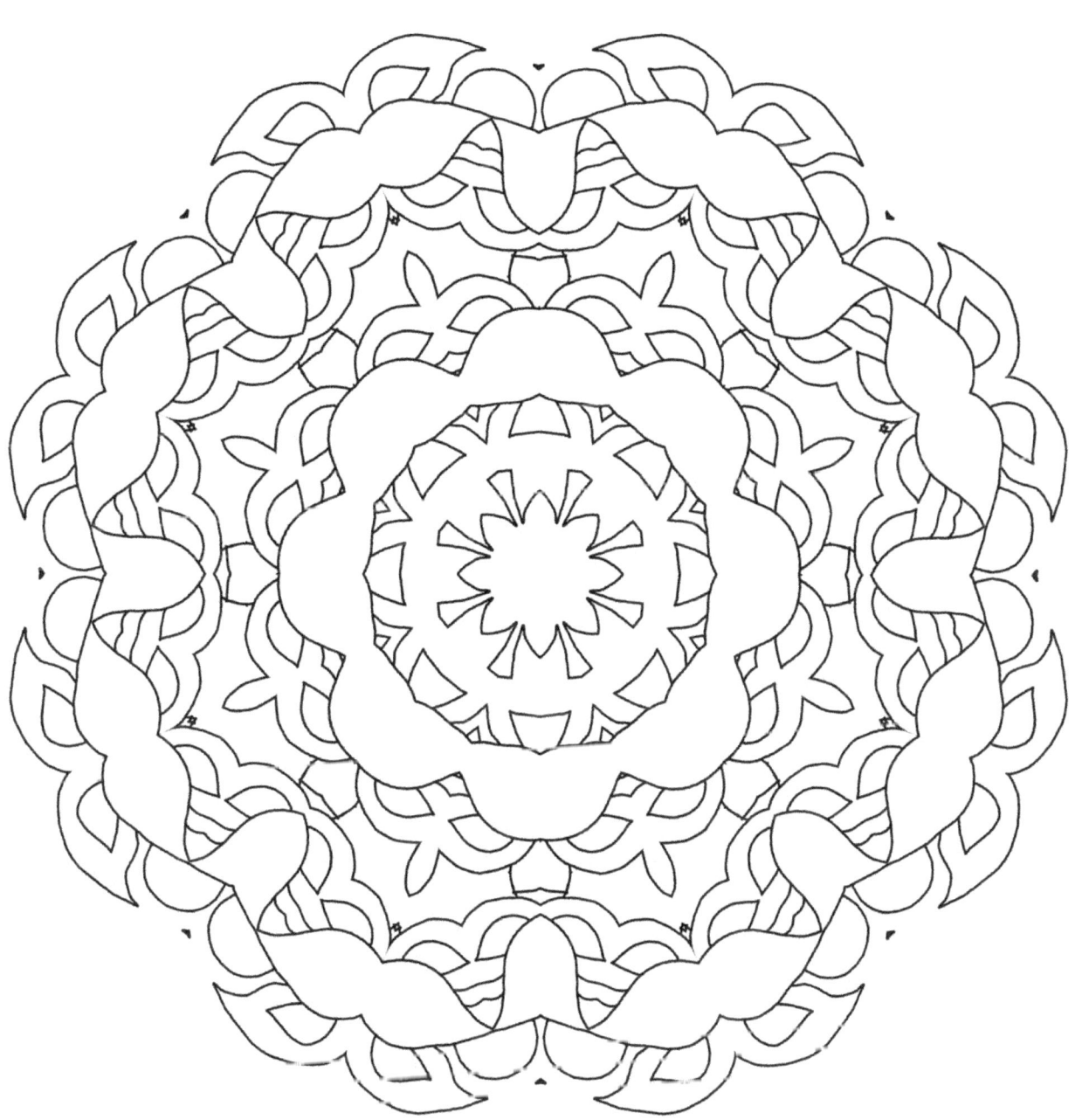

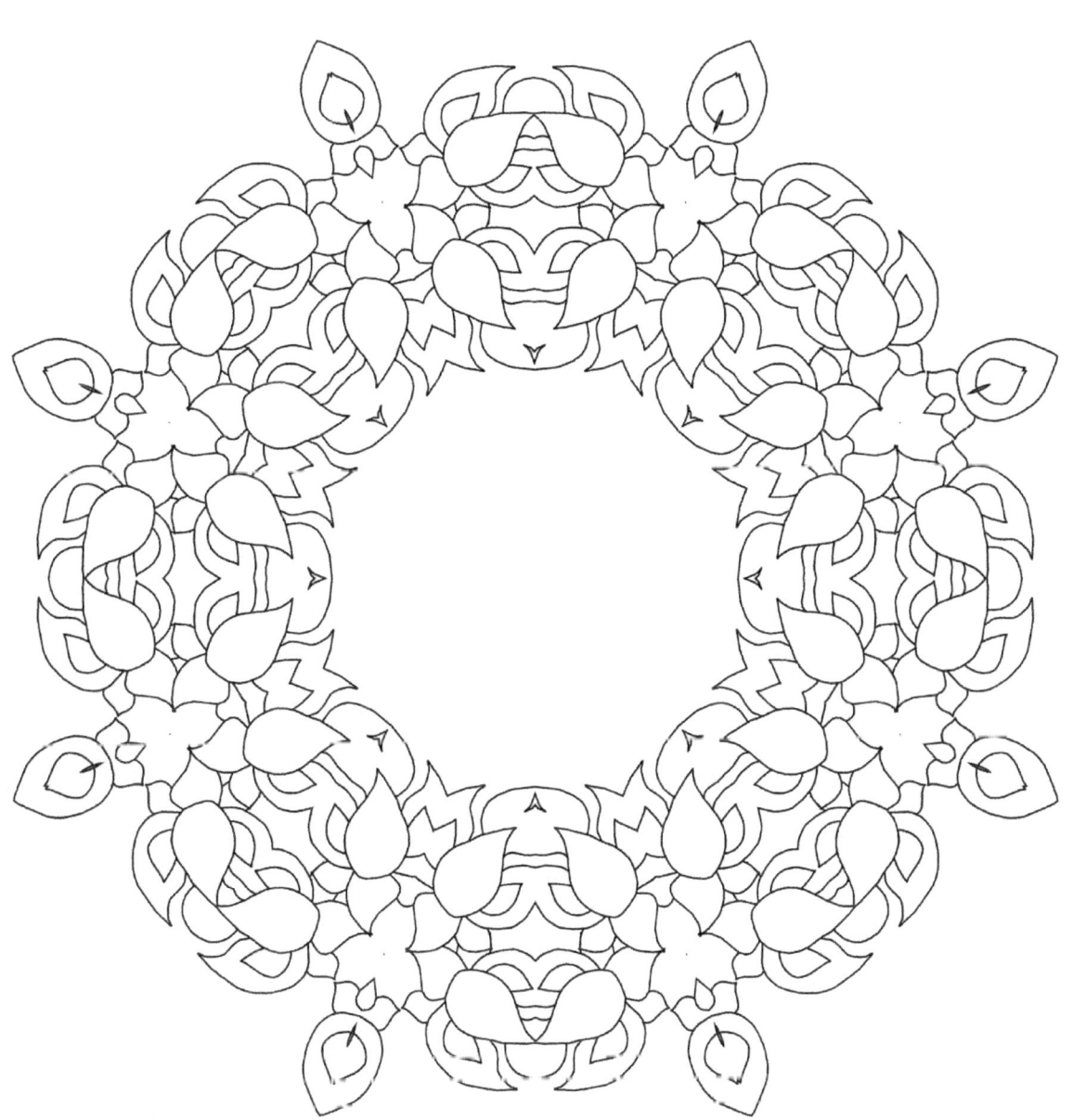

# Thank you

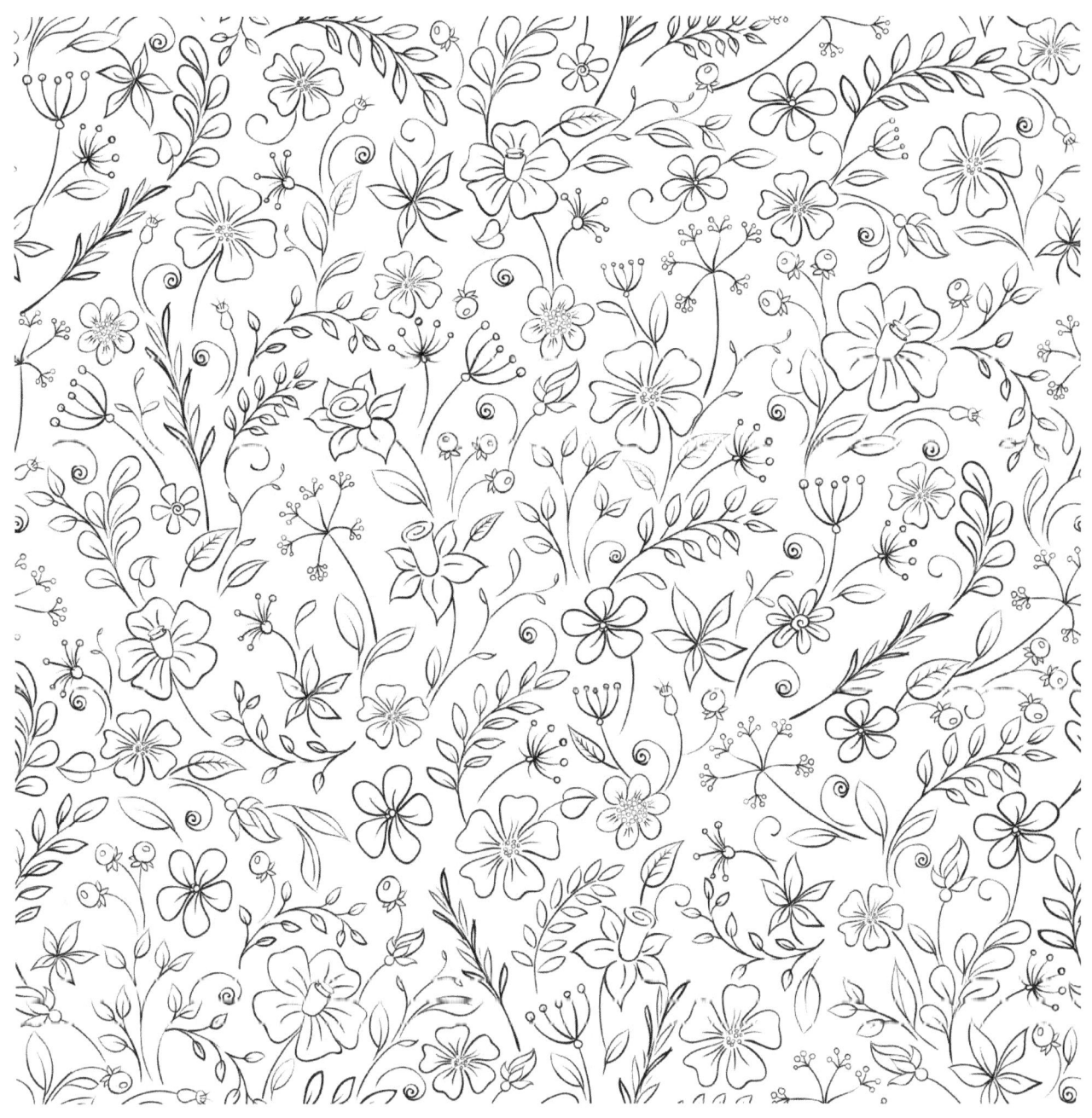

www.ingramcontent.com/pod-product-compliance
Lightning Source LLC
Chambersburg PA
CBHW081114180526
45170CB00008B/2846